NSO

OLYMPIAD WORKBOOK

6

NATIONAL SCIENCE OLYMPIAD

01	**Learning Objectives**
02	**Multiple Choice Questions**
03	**HOTS (Achievers Section)**
04	**Model Test Paper**
05	**Answer Keys and Solutions**
06	**OMR Answer Sheet**

V&S PUBLISHERS

Published by:

V&S PUBLISHERS

F-2/16, Ansari road, Daryaganj, New Delhi-110002
☎ 23240026, 23240027 • *Fax:* 011-23240028
✉ info@vspublishers.com • ⊕ www.vspublishers.com

Online Brandstore: amazon.in/vspublishers

Regional Office : Hyderabad
5-1-707/1, Brij Bhawan (Beside Central Bank of India Lane)
Bank Street, Koti, Hyderabad - 500 095
☎ 040-24737290
✉ vspublishershyd@gmail.com

Follow us on:   

BUY OUR BOOKS FROM: AMAZON FLIPKART

© **Copyright:** V&S PUBLISHERS
ISBN 978-81-977761-0-6
New Edition

<table>
<tr><td>

DISCLAIMER

</td></tr>
</table>

PUBLISHER'S NOTE

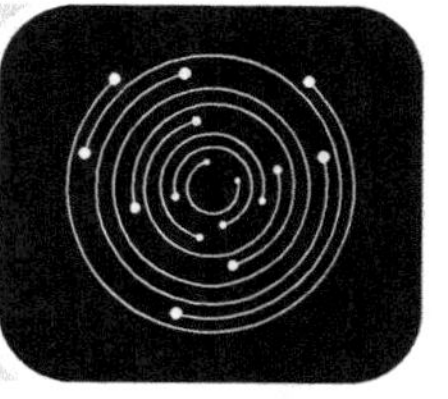

V&S Publishers has carved a significant niche in the publishing industry over the last decade, having successfully published more than 1000 titles across 9 languages spanning over 50 subject categories. Being known for the quality of content, we have built a reputation of excellence and reliability. We have consistently delivered **"Value & Substance"** to our readers, through a wide range of titles across a variety of genres covering school books, fiction and non-fiction that caters to different people from every section of the society.

The **Olympiad Guidebooks for classes 1-10** across all subjects, launched almost a decade ago, under the **GEN X Imprint**, became a go-to-source for the school students in no time, owing to their invaluable and substantive content written in a guidebook pattern,.

Having successfully sold a million copies of the same and in response to demand by both students as well as shopkeepers nationwide; we now present before you our newly launched **Olympiad Workbook Series**, designed for **classes 1-10 across 4 subjects**.

The workbooks are meticulously curated by a team of experienced educators, researchers and subject matter experts, edited by professionals and peer reviewed by teachers. The team has poured its efforts and expertise into creating a crisp and concise workbook which will help and guide the students to the path of success in Olympiad exams. The **MCQs** identified will not only help in scoring top marks in Olympiads but also inculcate a sense of deeper understanding of the subject, by way of solving **HOTS** and referring to complete solutions at the end of the book.

Here we present our new release– **OLYMPIAD WORKBOOK (NSO) CLASS–6** having following features:

- ☞ Based on the latest syllabi
- ☞ MCQs with comprehensive coverage of topics
- ☞ HOTS Questions liberally included
- ☞ A dedicated chapter on logical reasoning
- ☞ Model test paper for thorough practice
- ☞ Sample OMR sheet for real time simulation

We have made sure through our best efforts, that this workbook strictly follows the latest syllabi and patterns of the Olympiad Examination.

As **V&S Publishers** continuously strive to enhance the readability and maintain the credibility of our academic publications, we seek the support of our valuable readers in influencing and enriching the lives of future generations of students.

P.S. While every care has been taken to ensure the correctness of the content, if you come across any error, howsoever minor, do not hesitate to discuss with teachers while pointing that out to us in no uncertain terms.

We wish you all the best for your exams!

DISTINCTIVE FEATURES

01 Learning Objectives

They list the whole chapter as subtopics, helping the teachers to guide children in a step-by-step manner.

02 Multiple Choice Questions

MCQs act as an excellent learning aid, helping you to understand and work on your mistakes.

03 HOTS (Achievers Section)

The High Order Thinking Questions aim to help the student to solve Application-based questions and gain practical understanding of the subject.

04 Model Test Paper

Model test paper are provided at the end of each book, which help the student to test the knowledge which they have gained after thorough reading of all chapters.

05 Answer Key

Detailed Answer Key along with explanations aid the pupil to indentify, understand the mistakes they make during the course of Olympiad preparation.

CONTENTS

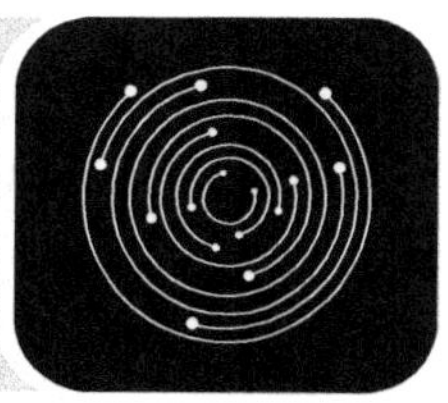

FOOD, HEALTH AND HYGIENE

LEARNING OBJECTIVES

➤ Food and its necessity
➤ Autotrophs and heterotrophs
➤ Components of food
➤ Functions of food
➤ Herbivores, carnivores and omnivores
➤ Health and hygiene

MULTIPLE CHOICE QUESTIONS

1. Read the following statements about diseases.
   i. They are caused by germs.
   ii. They are caused due to lack of nutrients in our diet.
   iii. They can be passed on to another person through contact.
   iv. They can be prevented by taking a balanced diet.

   Which pair of statements best describe a deficiency disease?
   (A) i and ii   (B) ii and iii
   (C) ii and iv   (D) i and iii

2. Calcium, iron, potassium, iodine and common salt are examples of __________.
   (A) Proteins   (B) Vitamins
   (C) Minerals   (D) Fats

3. Mosquitoes live on blood that they suck from humans and other animals. Mosquitoes and flies both come from the insect group. To which of the following categories do the mosquitoes and flies belong?
   (A) Omnivores, scavenger
   (B) Scavenger, parasite
   (C) Parasite, scavenger
   (D) Parasite, omnivores

4. Which vitamin is synthesised by bacteria in the intestine?
   (A) Vitamin E   (B) Vitamin K
   (C) Vitamin D   (D) Vitamin A

5. Green plants are known as producers. They prepare more food than they need. The extra food is stored in different parts of the plant. Identify the parts of the plant from which the following food items (W, X, Y and Z) are obtained and select the correct option.

Onion, potatoes	Spinach, Cabbage
W	X
Broccoli and Cauliflower	Rice and wheat flour
Y	Z

	W	X	Y	Z
(A)	Stem	Leaf	Flower	Seed
(B)	Fruit	Leaf	Flower	Seed
(C)	Leaf	Flower	Seed	Stem
(D)	Stem	Fruit	Leaf	Flower

6. The diagram below shows a simple food web.

Which animal is classified as an omnivore?

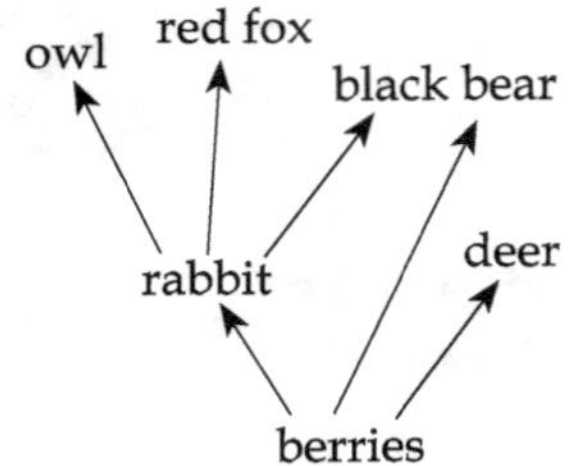

(A) Red fox   (B) Deer
(C) Black bear   (D) Rabbit

7. It is a form of malnutrition in which nutrients are oversupplied relative to the amounts required for normal growth, development and metabolism.
   I. What is this condition called?
   II. This condition will lead to __________.

	I	II
(A)	Malnutrition	Rickets
(B)	Overnutrition	Obesity
(C)	Overnutrition	Scurvy
(D)	Malnutrition	Kwashiorkor

8. Some beetles break down the remains of dead animals. Some mushrooms breakdown the remains of dead trees. How do these actions most benefit plants?
   (A) By returning nutrients to the soil
   (B) By releasing oxygen into the air
   (C) By making space for new animals
   (D) By decreasing the population of herbivores

9. The diagram below shows a simple food chain.

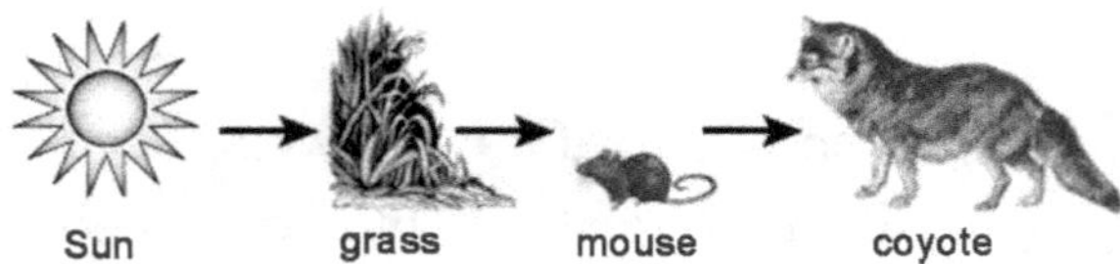

Which of the following animals might compete with the coyote in this food chain?

10. Which of the following food turns blue-black with iodine solution?
    (A) Onion   (B) Sugar
    (C) Potato   (D) Groundnut

11. Name the following:
    i. The nutrients which mainly give energy to our body.
    ii. The nutrients that are needed for the growth and maintenance of our body.
    iii. A vitamin required for maintaining good eyesight.
    iv. A mineral that is required for keeping our bones healthy.
    (A) (i) Proteins and fats,
        (ii) Proteins and minerals,
        (iii) Vitamin A,
        (iv) Calcium
    (B) (i) Proteins and minerals,
        (ii) Vitamin A,
        (iii) Calcium,
        (iv) Carbohydrates
    (C) (i) Fats,
        (ii) Proteins and minerals,
        (iii) Vitamin A,
        (iv) Calcium
    (D) (i) Carbohydrates and fats,
        (ii) Proteins and minerals,
        (iii) Vitamin A,
        (iv) Calcium

12. Basu lives in Delhi. One day Basu went to his ancestral village with his grandfather. He saw some people whose throats were somewhat swollen.

OLYMPIAD WORKBOOK (NSO) CLASS— 6

I. What is the name of this disease?

II. Which nutrient is lacking in the diets of the people who were suffering from the disease?

	I	II
(A)	Goitre	Iodine
(B)	PEM	Protein
(C)	Anemia	Iron
(D)	Scurvy	Vitamin

13. Read the following steps carefully.
    i.   Take few leaves of spinach.
    ii. Let a spinach leaf stand in the air for two days.
    iii. You will see that the spinach will wilt and grow smaller as the water in it dries up.

    What does the above experiment show?
    (A) Food is mostly fat
    (B) Food is mostly carbohydrates
    (C) Food is mostly water
    (D) Food is mostly proteins

14. When two drops of iodine solution are put on a substance, we get a blue-black colour. This indicates the presence of ___________.
    (A) Carbohydrates   (B) Starch
    (C) Fat   (D) Protein

15. It is said that water is vital for our body. Which of the following statements does not justify this statement?
    (A) It helps our body absorb nutrients from food
    (B) It serves as a solvent in which all chemical reactions take place in our body
    (C) It provides energy to our body
    (D) It transports nutrients throughout the body

16. The following parts of banana plant are used as food ___________.
    (A) Flower, leaf, stem
    (B) Fruit, stem, flower
    (C) Leaf, stem, fruit
    (D) Root, fruit, flower

17. An oily translucent patch on the paper shows that the food item contains _______.
    (A) Minerals
    (B) Carbohydrates
    (C) Proteins
    (D) Fat

18. Match Column I with Column II, and choose the correct option.

Column I	Column II
i. Herbivores	a. Are animal product
ii. Lions and tigers	b. Are vegetables
iii. Milk, curd, paneer, ghee	c. Eat other animals
iv. Spinach, cauliflower, carrot	d. Eat plants and plant products

    (A) i-b, ii-a, iii-d, iv-c
    (B) i-d, ii-c, iii-a, iv-b
    (C) i- c, ii-a, iii-d, iv-b
    (D) i-b, ii-d-iii- a, iv-c

19. The colour of an egg is dependent on the ___________.
    (A) Breed of the hen
    (B) Diet of the hen
    (C) Shape of the egg
    (D) Variety of the egg

20. The food items shown in the figure are rich in nutrient X.

Read the given statements regarding the nutrient X.

i. When we grow, our body needs X to make new cells.

ii. X is also needed to replace old and damaged cells.

iii. Growing children and sick people require less amount of X in their diet.

iv. The total requirement of X for an adult is about 100–103 grams per day.

Which of the above statements are incorrect?

(A) (i) and (iv)

(B) (iii) and (iv)

(C) (ii) and (iii)

(D) (i) and (ii)

21. Reeta eats following foods in her diet.

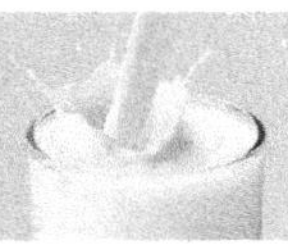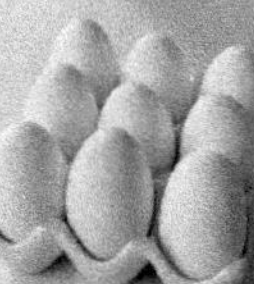

In her diet which of the following food category and nutrient is she is lacking in?

(A) Protective foods, mineral

(B) Protective foods, vitamins

(C) Protective foods, vitamins and minerals

(D) Body building, vitamins and minerals

Direction for question 22.

Coyotes, willows, squirrels and snowshoe hares are all part of a particular forest ecosystem.

22. Which of the following food chains is possible for the organisms in this forest?

(A) Sun → Coyote → Snowshoe hare → Willow

(B) Sun → Willow → Snowshoe hare → Coyote

(C) Sun → Squirrel → Snowshoe hare → Coyote

(D) Sun → Willow → Snowshoe hare → Squirrel

23. Identify a food product that has a micronutrient added to it.

	Food	Micronutrient(s) added
(A)	Sweet porridge	Folic acid, vitamins, and calcium
(B)	Mango shake	Vitamin D, Vitamin A
(C)	Salty khichdi	Iodine
(D)	Some juices	Calcium

24. My favourite food is chocolate. If I eat only chocolates for a long period of time, ________________________________. [Children are encouraged to incorporate a wide variety of foods in their diet to make sure that they get adequate nutrition.]

Which of the following sentence is correct for completing above sentence?

(A) I may become deficient in several macronutrients

(B) I may become deficient in several macro and micronutrients

(C) I may become deficient in several micronutrients

(D) I may become deficient in protein

25. Choose the correct option:

I. Name the nutrient which mainly gives energy to our body.

II. Name the vitamin required for maintaining good eye sight.

	I	II
(A)	Fat	Vitamin B
(B)	Proteins	Vitamin A
(C)	Vitamins	Vitamin A
(D)	Fats	Vitamin A

26. Which one of the following food items is likely to contain the most bacteria?

(A) Frozen raw chicken

(B) Recently cooked chicken

(C) An opened can of a fizzy drink

(D) Bottled mayonnaise

27. What are the basic steps for washing hands?

(A) Wash thoroughly with water and dry

(B) Apply soap, wash thoroughly, rinse and use paper towels

(C) Apply soap, wash thoroughly

(D) Wash thoroughly with water

28. Choose the correct option:

i. Rice alone is sufficient to provide all nutrients to the body.

ii. Deficiency diseases can be prevented by eating a balanced diet.

iii. Balanced diet for the body should contain a variety of food items.

iv. Meat alone is sufficient to provide all nutrients to the body.

(A) i and ii

(B) ii and iii

(C) iii only

(D) i and iv

29. The food items shown in the figure are sources of mainly ___________.

(A) Fats

(B) Carbohydrates

(C) Vitamins

(D) Proteins

30. Match the following:

(A)	Vitamin C	(i)	Goitre
(B)	Vitamin A	(ii)	Scurvy
(C)	Iodine	(iii)	Bone decay
(D)	Calcium	(iv)	Loss of vision

(A) (A) - (iii); (B) - (iv); (C) - (ii); (D) - (i)

(B) (A) - (ii); (B) - (iv); (C) - (i); (D) - (iii)

(C) (A) - (ii); (B) - (iii); (C) - (i); (D) - (iv)

(D) (A) - (i); (B) - (ii); (C) - (iii); (D) - (iv)

31. Take small amount of food sample in a test tube. Put a few drops of iodine on it. Note down the change in colour. Bluish black colour indicates the presence of (A). The food product (B) can be used for this experiment.

    Choose the correct option from 'a' and 'b' and answer the question.

	a	b
(A)	Calcium	Bread
(B)	Starch	Potato
(C)	Proteins	Dals
(D)	Vitamin C	Orange

32. White of an egg turns violet when two drops of copper sulphate and ten drops of caustic soda are added to it. This indicates the presence of which of the following components of food?
    (A) Starch
    (B) Proteins
    (C) Fats
    (D) Vitamins

33. Which of the following options contain a healthy diet?
    (A) A variety of foods each day, such as fruits and vegetables, whole grain bread and cereal, meat, dairy products, dry peas, beans, nuts and water.
    (B) Fat and cholesterol are found in meat, egg, butter, cream and liver.
    (C) Vegetables, deep fried food such as potato chips and alcoholic drinks.
    (D) Snacks, candy and soft drinks.

34. Which food items from the given choices should be included in our diet to protect us from bleeding gums?
    (A) Cheese
    (B) Yeast
    (C) Amla
    (D) Wheat germ

35. People of Rajasthan eat roots of khijri trees during
    (A) festivals
    (B) drought
    (C) flood
    (D) None of these

1.	Ⓐ Ⓑ Ⓒ Ⓓ	8.	Ⓐ Ⓑ Ⓒ Ⓓ	15.	Ⓐ Ⓑ Ⓒ Ⓓ	22	Ⓐ Ⓑ Ⓒ Ⓓ	29.	Ⓐ Ⓑ Ⓒ Ⓓ
2.	Ⓐ Ⓑ Ⓒ Ⓓ	9.	Ⓐ Ⓑ Ⓒ Ⓓ	16.	Ⓐ Ⓑ Ⓒ Ⓓ	23.	Ⓐ Ⓑ Ⓒ Ⓓ	30.	Ⓐ Ⓑ Ⓒ Ⓓ
3.	Ⓐ Ⓑ Ⓒ Ⓓ	10.	Ⓐ Ⓑ Ⓒ Ⓓ	17.	Ⓐ Ⓑ Ⓒ Ⓓ	24.	Ⓐ Ⓑ Ⓒ Ⓓ	31.	Ⓐ Ⓑ Ⓒ Ⓓ
4.	Ⓐ Ⓑ Ⓒ Ⓓ	11.	Ⓐ Ⓑ Ⓒ Ⓓ	18.	Ⓐ Ⓑ Ⓒ Ⓓ	25.	Ⓐ Ⓑ Ⓒ Ⓓ	32.	Ⓐ Ⓑ Ⓒ Ⓓ
5.	Ⓐ Ⓑ Ⓒ Ⓓ	12.	Ⓐ Ⓑ Ⓒ Ⓓ	19.	Ⓐ Ⓑ Ⓒ Ⓓ	26.	Ⓐ Ⓑ Ⓒ Ⓓ	33.	Ⓐ Ⓑ Ⓒ Ⓓ
6.	Ⓐ Ⓑ Ⓒ Ⓓ	13.	Ⓐ Ⓑ Ⓒ Ⓓ	20.	Ⓐ Ⓑ Ⓒ Ⓓ	27.	Ⓐ Ⓑ Ⓒ Ⓓ	34.	Ⓐ Ⓑ Ⓒ Ⓓ
7.	Ⓐ Ⓑ Ⓒ Ⓓ	14.	Ⓐ Ⓑ Ⓒ Ⓓ	21.	Ⓐ Ⓑ Ⓒ Ⓓ	28.	Ⓐ Ⓑ Ⓒ Ⓓ	35.	Ⓐ Ⓑ Ⓒ Ⓓ

FIBRE TO FABRIC

LEARNING OBJECTIVES

➤ Different types of fibres
➤ Characteristics of different types of fibres
➤ The ways in which fibres are extracted from plants and animals

MULTIPLE CHOICE QUESTIONS

1. Cotton is the most desirable fabric for making undergarments because it is __________.
   (A) Absorbent   (B) Dull
   (C) Shining   (D) Strong

2. Which fabric has a dull surface?
   (A) Nylon   (B) Polyester
   (C) Silk   (D) Wool

3. Which of the following fabrics does not take stains easily?
   (A) Cotton   (B) Silk
   (C) Wool   (D) Synthetic

4. The natural fibres are obtained from __________.
   (A) Plants
   (B) Animals
   (C) Plants and animals both
   (D) Neither from plants nor animals

5. Nylon and polyester are obtained from __________.
   (A) Plants
   (B) Animals
   (C) Both
   (D) From chemical substances

6. An experiment that tests dye fixation on a 100% cotton-woven fabric would examine which of the following properties?
   (A) Easily washable
   (B) Water repellence
   (C) Abrasion resistance
   (D) Moisture absorption

7. Which of the following does not yield wool?
   (A) Yak   (B) Camel
   (C) Goat   (D) Woolly dog

8. The rearing of silkworms to obtain silk is called __________.
   (A) Sericulture   (B) Horticulture
   (C) Agriculture   (D) Aqua-culture

9. Cotton bolls are developed from the __________.
   (A) Seeds   (B) Leaves
   (C) Flowers   (D) None of these

10. Silk fibre obtained from silk moth is __________.
    (A) Carbohydrate   (B) Fat
    (C) Protein   (D) Sugars

11. Silkworms are reared on __________.
    (A) Mulberry plants (B) Mango plants
    (C) Money plants   (D) None of these

12. Part of the jute plant that is used to make cloth is the __________.
    (A) Stem   (B) Root
    (C) Leaf   (D) Flower

13. Which fabric is made of staple fibre?
    - (A) Cotton
    - (B) Nylon
    - (C) Polyester
    - (D) Silk

14. Which of these is not a property of jute?
    - (A) Biodegradability
    - (B) Durability
    - (C) Smoothness
    - (D) Strength

15. Which of these do you think traps the most air?
    - (A) Nylon
    - (B) Cotton
    - (C) Wool
    - (D) Polyester

16. Ananya, Ranchit, Sanchit and Soni are talking about wool and silk. Who among them is correct?
    - (A) Ananya: Silk doesn't need to be detangled like wool because silk is obtained directly as thread from cocoon
    - (B) Ranchit: Silk doesn't need to be detangled like wool because thread from a single cocoon can be used as yarn directly
    - (C) Sanchit: Silk doesn't need to be detangled like wool because silk fibre is stronger than wool
    - (D) Soni: Ananya and Ranchit are correct

17. Can all the fleece of a sheep be used to make wool?
    - (A) Yes
    - (B) No, sheep stays dirty which makes some fleece useless
    - (C) Yes, it can be done in case of a few sheep
    - (D) No, sheep has hair of different thicknesses and quality like us. Only some of them can be used to make wool

18. Identify P in the given Venn diagram __________.

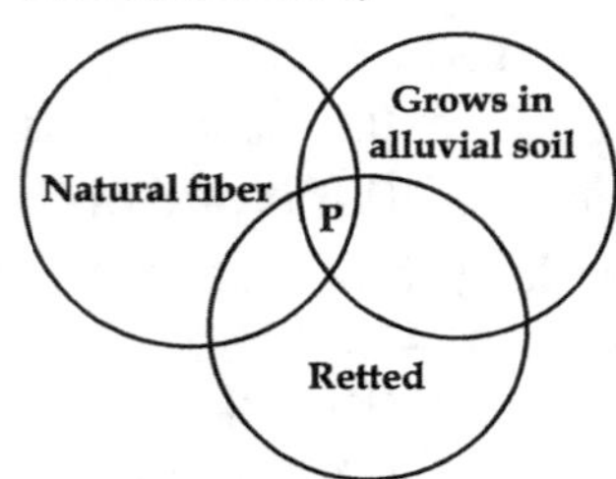

19. The harvesting of which natural fiber includes rippling, retting, and scutching __________.
    - (A) Cotton
    - (B) Linen
    - (C) Wool
    - (D) Silk

20. What does filament mean?
    - (A) A process to add bulk to a fiber
    - (B) Fibrous chemical found in all plants
    - (C) Long, continuous strands measured in yards or meters
    - (D) The main component of plants

21. Which of the following is a correct difference between weaving and knitting?
    - (A) Weaving is the process of interlacing two sets of yarns at right angles to each other to form a fabric while knitting is inter looping of one or more set of yarns
    - (B) Weaving is done for silk only while knitting is done for wools only
    - (C) Weaving is done with machines while knitting is done by hand
    - (D) All of them

22. Refer to the following Venn diagram. Which of these characteristics can be represented by P?

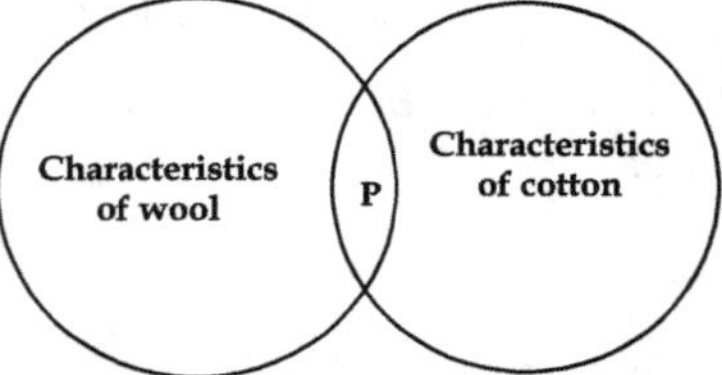

    - (A) Comfortable to wear in hot and humid weather
    - (B) Ability to trap and retain water
    - (C) Fluffy texture
    - (D) Natural fibers

23. Cotton is stronger when it is wet. This is because of __________.
    - (A) Crystalline fiber
    - (B) Hydrophilic in nature
    - (C) Cellulose layer
    - (D) All of them

18 and 19 options list (first column top):
- (A) Jute
- (B) Silk
- (C) Wool
- (D) Nylon

24. Satin weave fabrics are ___________.
(A) Durable
(B) Cheap
(C) Expensive
(D) Dull

25. Rehan wants to check the fiber type of a piece of cloth to find out if it's a natural or synthetic one. He performed burn test to solve that purpose in the following steps:
   i.   Rehan pulled a small snippet from the seam allowance or the end of yarn.
   ii. He held it with a pair of tweezers, put a flame to the end and then pulled it away.
   iii. He saw that it continued to burn after the flame was removed.

   Identify the fiber now:
   (A) Wool
   (B) Synthetic
   (C) Cotton
   (D) Silk

26. Select the correct statement from the following
   (A) Jute is obtained from stem of the jute plant
   (B) Coir obtained from coconut is a weak fiber
   (C) The process of making yarn from fiber is called weaving
   (D) Both (A) and (B)

27. Which of the following can be used as an unstitched piece of fabric?
   (A) Dhoti
   (B) Turban
   (C) Skirt
   (D) Both (A) and (B)

28. I am sometimes referred to as the "workhorse" fiber of the industry. My strength reinforces the cotton fibers. Who am I?
   (A) Synthetic fiber
   (B) Polyester fiber
   (C) Flax fiber
   (D) Jute fiber

29. In case of man-made fibres, this process is done by three different methods (wet, dry, melt).
   (A) Washing
   (B) Cleaning
   (C) Spinning
   (D) Both (A) and (B)

30. Look at the picture below. He is a football player named Lionel Messi. Which fiber-made clothing he wears while playing football?

   (A) Asbestos clothing
   (B) Fur
   (C) Protective padding
   (D) Robes

31. The thin strand of __________ that we see, are made up of still thinner strand called __________.

    (A) Fiber, yarn
    (B) Fiber fabrics
    (C) Fabrics, fiber
    (D) Yarn, fibers

32. Swati, Sanchit, Surbhi and Sakshi were talking about the difference between the weaving and knitting.

    Who among them correctly made the difference between weaving and knitting?

    (A) Swati: The process of making a yarn from fibers is called knitting. And weaving is interlacing of two sets of yarns at right angles to make a fabric

    (B) Sanchit: The process of making a yarn from fibers is called weaving. And knitting is interlacing of two sets of yarns at right angles to make a fabric. Weaving is done on looms

    (C) Surbhi: Weaving is interlacing of two sets of yarns at right angles to make a fabric. In the knitting process, the thread or yarn is used to create a cloth

    (D) Sakshi: Weaving is done for silk only while knitting is done for wool only

33. Following points shows the characteristics of fibres. Fabric made from above fibre is comfortable to use during which of the following seasons?
    - Allow free movement of air.
    - High water absorption capacity.

    (A) Winter season
    (B) Spring season
    (C) Summer season
    (D) Rainy season

34. At which of the following stages will bleaching and dyeing (addition of colours) be usually done?

    (A) Just before the fabrics are made.
    (B) After the fabrics are made.
    (C) Before the yarns are made.
    (D) After the yarns are made.

35. Which of the following materials is used to make gloves for electricians?

    (A) Silk
    (B) Wool
    (C) Rubber
    (D) Cotton

—Darken Your Choice with HB Pencil—

1.	Ⓐ Ⓑ Ⓒ Ⓓ	8.	Ⓐ Ⓑ Ⓒ Ⓓ	15.	Ⓐ Ⓑ Ⓒ Ⓓ	22	Ⓐ Ⓑ Ⓒ Ⓓ	29.	Ⓐ Ⓑ Ⓒ Ⓓ
2.	Ⓐ Ⓑ Ⓒ Ⓓ	9.	Ⓐ Ⓑ Ⓒ Ⓓ	16.	Ⓐ Ⓑ Ⓒ Ⓓ	23.	Ⓐ Ⓑ Ⓒ Ⓓ	30.	Ⓐ Ⓑ Ⓒ Ⓓ
3.	Ⓐ Ⓑ Ⓒ Ⓓ	10.	Ⓐ Ⓑ Ⓒ Ⓓ	17.	Ⓐ Ⓑ Ⓒ Ⓓ	24.	Ⓐ Ⓑ Ⓒ Ⓓ	31.	Ⓐ Ⓑ Ⓒ Ⓓ
4.	Ⓐ Ⓑ Ⓒ Ⓓ	11.	Ⓐ Ⓑ Ⓒ Ⓓ	18.	Ⓐ Ⓑ Ⓒ Ⓓ	25.	Ⓐ Ⓑ Ⓒ Ⓓ	32.	Ⓐ Ⓑ Ⓒ Ⓓ
5.	Ⓐ Ⓑ Ⓒ Ⓓ	12.	Ⓐ Ⓑ Ⓒ Ⓓ	19.	Ⓐ Ⓑ Ⓒ Ⓓ	26.	Ⓐ Ⓑ Ⓒ Ⓓ	33.	Ⓐ Ⓑ Ⓒ Ⓓ
6.	Ⓐ Ⓑ Ⓒ Ⓓ	13.	Ⓐ Ⓑ Ⓒ Ⓓ	20.	Ⓐ Ⓑ Ⓒ Ⓓ	27.	Ⓐ Ⓑ Ⓒ Ⓓ	34.	Ⓐ Ⓑ Ⓒ Ⓓ
7.	Ⓐ Ⓑ Ⓒ Ⓓ	14.	Ⓐ Ⓑ Ⓒ Ⓓ	21.	Ⓐ Ⓑ Ⓒ Ⓓ	28.	Ⓐ Ⓑ Ⓒ Ⓓ	35.	Ⓐ Ⓑ Ⓒ Ⓓ

SORTING AND SEPARATION OF MATERIALS

LEARNING OBJECTIVES

➤ Materials and its classification
➤ Need to separate substances
➤ Water as a solvent
➤ Significance of classification of objects
➤ Various means of separating materials

MULTIPLE CHOICE QUESTIONS

1. The rate of sedimentation is increased by adding _________ to the water.
   (A) Salt
   (B) Sugar
   (C) Alum
   (D) Soap

2. The process followed to separate grains from the stalks is called
   (A) Winnowing
   (B) Threshing
   (C) Sieving
   (D) Handpicking

3. Look at the picture below and find out the method by which components in the mixture are separated.

   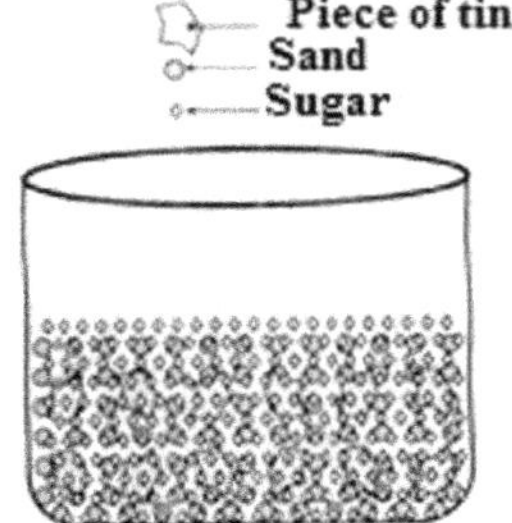

   (A) Handpicking
   (B) Winnowing
   (C) Threshing
   (D) Sieving

4. When a bottle of soda water is opened, carbon dioxide escapes, producing a fizz. This is due to:
   (A) A decrease in the solubility with a decrease in temperature
   (B) A decrease in the solubility on decreasing pressure and temperature
   (C) A decrease in the solubility on increasing the quantity
   (D) A decrease in the solubility on decreasing the quantity

5. Butter is separated from curd by the process of:
   (A) Filtration
   (B) Heating
   (C) Churning
   (D) Sieving

6. Which of the following is not characteristic of solids?
   (A) High rigidity
   (B) Regular shape
   (C) High density
   (D) High compressibility

7. When we blow air into the balloon, it inflates because:
   (A) Air particles diffuse into the balloon
   (B) Air particles collide with the walls of the balloon and exert pressure on them
   (C) Rubber is elastic in nature
   (D) The temperature of air in the balloon increases

8. Select a good conductor of heat among the following options.
   (A) Glass (B) Graphite
   (C) Rubber (D) Wood

9. The process in which particles of a solid settle down in a liquid is known as:
   (A) Sublimation (B) Precipitation
   (C) Decantation (D) Sedimentation

10. Which of the following is essential to perform winnowing activity?
   (A) Soil (B) Wind
   (C) Water (D) None of these

11. Handpicking method is effective in:
   (A) Solid mixtures
   (B) Liquid mixtures
   (C) Gaseous mixtures
   (D) None of these

12. Which of the following is an example of irreversible change?
   (A) Freezing water to make ice
   (B) Boiling water
   (C) Baking a cake
   (D) Breaking glass

13. The picture below shows a mixture of beads and flour in a bowl.

   Rehan wants to separate the beads from the flour in the bowl. What separation method can he use?
   (A) Handpicking
   (B) Threshing
   (C) Winnowing
   (D) Sieving

14. Saimaa is making herself a cup of coffee. She adds in sugar to her coffee. What will happen if she continues adding more coffee powder to her drink?
   (A) The coffee powder will continue dissolving in the water
   (B) The coffee powder will not dissolve in the water. The coffee solution will reach a stage where no more solid (coffee powder) can dissolve. The solution will become saturated
   (C) The solution will become unsaturated
   (D) None of these

15. Which of the following is incorrect?
   (A) Solids that can dissolve in a liquid are said to be soluble in that liquid
   (B) When a solid dissolves in a liquid, the resulting mixture is known as a solution
   (C) When a solid is added to a liquid and the liquid changes colour, it means that the solid is soluble
   (D) It is impossible to change the rate at which a solid dissolves in a liquid

16. Study the picture below and answer the questions that follow.

   What is the name of the process taking place in the picture?
   (A) Loading
   (B) Filtration
   (C) Sedimentation
   (D) Evaporation

17. The picture below shows a teabag in a glass of water. What is the function of the teabag?

OLYMPIAD WORKBOOK (NSO) CLASS— 6

(A) The teabag acts as a sieve which allows water to pass through, but keeps the tea leaves in the bag

(B) The teabag acts as a filter which allows water to pass through, but keeps the tea leaves in the bag

(C) The teabag acts as a filter which allows water to pass through, but sediment the tea leaves in the bag

(D) The teabag acts as a decanter which allows water to pass through

18. Fill in the blanks below, using the helping words provided in the box. Each word can be used only once.

filtration, soluble, permanent, substance, reversible, temporary

1. When a sliced apple turns brown, a new _____________ has formed.

2. Burning plastic is a _____________ change.

3. We can separate insoluble solids from liquids by _____________.

4. A _____________ change takes place when a material that has undergone a change can return to its original form.

5. When a solid is able to dissolve in water, we say that it is _____________ in water.

6. A change is _____________ when no new substances are formed.

Choose the correct sequence:

(A) Permanent, filtration, substance, reversible, soluble, temporary

(B) Substance, permanent, filtration, reversible, soluble, temporary

(C) Permanent, filtration, reversible, substance, soluble, temporary

(D) Soluble, temporary, permanent, filtration, reversible, substance

19. Samarth mixed the following things in a bowl, then carried out the following steps.

Which two steps are not in a correct sequence?

Step 1: Remove the pencils by sorting them by hand.

Step 2: Use a magnet to separate the iron nails.

Step 3: Pour water into the mixture of sand and sugar.

Step 4: Remove the copper nails by sorting by hand, or by using a sieve.

Step 5: Use filtration to separate the sand.

Step 6: Use evaporation to obtain the sugar.

(A) 1 and 2   (B) 2 and 3

(C) 5 and 6   (D) 3 and 4

20. Match the objects given below with the materials from which they could be made. Remember, an object could be made from more than one material and a given material could be used for making many objects.

Objects	Materials
1. Book	Plastic
2. Shoes	Wood
3. Toy	Glass
4. Chair	Leather
5. Tumbler	Paper

Choose the correct sequence

(A) Wood, leather, plastic, paper, glass

(B) Paper, leather, wood, plastic, glass

(C) Wood, plastic, glass, paper, leather

(D) Leather, wood, plastic, paper, glass

21. Select the correct option.
   (A) Stone is transparent, while glass is opaque
   (B) A notebook has lustre while an eraser does not
   (C) A piece of wood floats on water
   (D) Chalk dissolves in water

22. A pure substance is one which ________.
   (A) Is made up of only one type of particles
   (B) Has a uniform texture throughout
   (C) Has a fixed boiling point or melting point
   (D) All of these

23. Salt is obtained from sea water by using which of the following processes?
   (A) Centrifugation   (B) Condensation
   (C) Sedimentation   (D) Evaporation

24. Two solids are separated by winnowing depending on ________.
   (A) Difference in their colours
   (B) Difference in their sizes
   (C) Difference in their weights
   (D) Difference in their odours

25. A mixture of wheat and husk can be separated by ________.
   (A) Filtration   (B) Decantation
   (C) Winnowing   (D) Evaporation

26. Mariam is a housewife. She lives in a small town. She has gone to visit her village house. Prior to her departure, she kept her utensils, crockeries, chopper, spoons, etc. under lock and key. She returned home after a few days. She saw that there was deposition of brown colour on her chopper. The cooking pots, spoons, remained the same as they were. Of the crockeries, some are made of metal and some are of non-metals.

What is the name of brown coloured coating on the chopper and knife?
   (A) Soil   (B) Rust
   (C) Iron   (D) Both (B) and (C)

27. The sequence of steps for separating a mixture of salt, sand and camphor is ________.
   (A) Adding water, filtration, evaporation, sublimation
   (B) Adding water, filtration, sublimation, evaporation
   (C) Sublimation, adding water, filtration, evaporation
   (D) Sublimation, adding water, evaporation, filtration

28. A solution which cannot dissolve more of a given substance at a given temperature is ________.
   (A) A saturated solution
   (B) A filtrate
   (C) A solution
   (D) An unsaturated solution

29. Sam's father prepared paneer from curdled milk. Which method did he use to separate paneer from curdled milk?
   (A) Condensation   (B) Filtration
   (C) Evaporation   (D) Sedimentation

30. Study the following flowchart and find out what X, Y and Z could be.

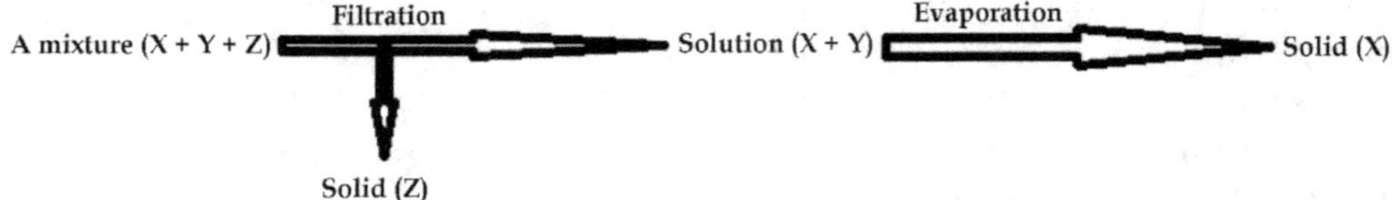

   (A) Sugar, water, sawdust
   (B) Sawdust water, sugar
   (C) Chalk powder, water, sawdust
   (D) Salt, water, sugar

OLYMPIAD WORKBOOK (NSO) CLASS— 6

31. If opacity is the distinct feature of wood, then what is glass known for in the same way?
    (A) Its transparency
    (B) Its magnetic nature
    (C) Its conductivity to heat
    (D) Its lustrous nature

32. When Amrita was asked to pick up a few articles from a collection, she picked up the following:
    ■ Wooden scale
    ■ Glass test tube
    ■ Paper basket
    Which of the following articles is she most likely to pick up the next?
    (A) Steel cup   (B) Iron chain
    (C) Rubber gloves   (D) Copper wire

33. Which characteristics given below are of metals?
    (i)   They are hard.
    (ii) They have lustre.
    (iii) They are good conductors of electricity
    (A) Only (i) and (ii)
    (B) Only (ii) and (iii)
    (C) Only (i) and (iii)
    (D) (i), (ii) and (iii)

34. Clinical thermometers are made of glass. Identify the characteristic(s) considered for the selection.
    (i)   It is a bad conductor of heat
    (ii) It is transparent
    (iii) It is strong
    (A) Only (i) and (ii)
    (B) Only (ii) and (iii)
    (C) Only (i) and (iii)
    (D) (i), (ii) and (iii)

35. Suresh put the same things in two different bags X and Y. However bag Y could not hold all the items and got torn?

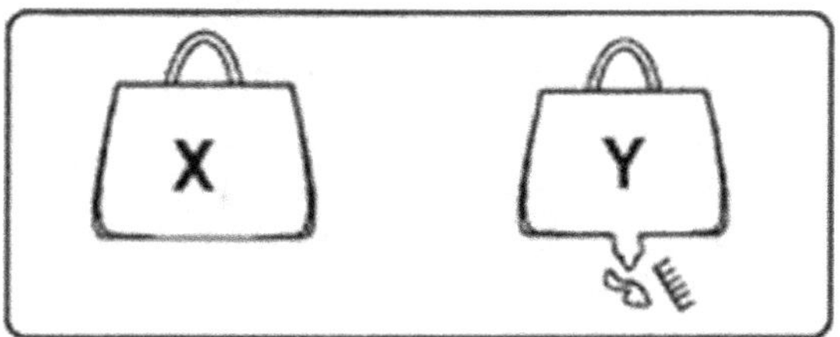

    What did Suresh conclude?
    (A) Bag X is more flexible than bag T.
    (B) Bag T is lighter than bag X
    (C) Bag T is softer than bag X.
    (D) Bag X is stronger than bag T.

—Darken Your Choice with HB Pencil—

1.	Ⓐ Ⓑ Ⓒ Ⓓ	8.	Ⓐ Ⓑ Ⓒ Ⓓ	15.	Ⓐ Ⓑ Ⓒ Ⓓ	22	Ⓐ Ⓑ Ⓒ Ⓓ	29.	Ⓐ Ⓑ Ⓒ Ⓓ
2.	Ⓐ Ⓑ Ⓒ Ⓓ	9.	Ⓐ Ⓑ Ⓒ Ⓓ	16.	Ⓐ Ⓑ Ⓒ Ⓓ	23.	Ⓐ Ⓑ Ⓒ Ⓓ	30.	Ⓐ Ⓑ Ⓒ Ⓓ
3.	Ⓐ Ⓑ Ⓒ Ⓓ	10.	Ⓐ Ⓑ Ⓒ Ⓓ	17.	Ⓐ Ⓑ Ⓒ Ⓓ	24.	Ⓐ Ⓑ Ⓒ Ⓓ	31.	Ⓐ Ⓑ Ⓒ Ⓓ
4.	Ⓐ Ⓑ Ⓒ Ⓓ	11.	Ⓐ Ⓑ Ⓒ Ⓓ	18.	Ⓐ Ⓑ Ⓒ Ⓓ	25.	Ⓐ Ⓑ Ⓒ Ⓓ	32.	Ⓐ Ⓑ Ⓒ Ⓓ
5.	Ⓐ Ⓑ Ⓒ Ⓓ	12.	Ⓐ Ⓑ Ⓒ Ⓓ	19.	Ⓐ Ⓑ Ⓒ Ⓓ	26.	Ⓐ Ⓑ Ⓒ Ⓓ	33.	Ⓐ Ⓑ Ⓒ Ⓓ
6.	Ⓐ Ⓑ Ⓒ Ⓓ	13.	Ⓐ Ⓑ Ⓒ Ⓓ	20.	Ⓐ Ⓑ Ⓒ Ⓓ	27.	Ⓐ Ⓑ Ⓒ Ⓓ	34.	Ⓐ Ⓑ Ⓒ Ⓓ
7.	Ⓐ Ⓑ Ⓒ Ⓓ	14.	Ⓐ Ⓑ Ⓒ Ⓓ	21.	Ⓐ Ⓑ Ⓒ Ⓓ	28.	Ⓐ Ⓑ Ⓒ Ⓓ	35.	Ⓐ Ⓑ Ⓒ Ⓓ

CHANGES AROUND US

LEARNING OBJECTIVES

➤ The difference between reversible and irreversible changes
➤ Physical and chemical changes
➤ Changes that happen when different substances are mixed

MULTIPLE CHOICE QUESTIONS

1. Which of the following is a reversible change?
   (A) Melting of ice
   (B) Burning of matchstick
   (C) Changing of milk into curd
   (D) Germination of seed

2. In a chemical change _____________.
   (A) The molecules of the substance do not change
   (B) The molecules of the substance change
   (C) The substance remains same
   (D) Change is reversible

3. Which of the following is an example of physical change?
   (A) A bud turning into a flower
   (B) Rusting of iron
   (C) Ripening of fruit
   (D) Boiling of water

4. In a chemical change _____________.
   (A) Energy is either absorbed or given out
   (B) Energy is always absorbed
   (C) Energy is given out
   (D) Energy changes do not occur

5. While making a wooden wheel, the iron rim is made slightly smaller than wooden wheel. Why? Choose the correct option.
   (A) Because on heating the rim, the iron expands. The wooden wheel is then put in the rim in its expanded state. On cooling, the iron rim contracts and fits tightly with the wooden wheel
   (B) Because the iron expands on cooling
   (C) Because the wooden wheel contracts on heating
   (D) All of them

6. Electric wires or telephone wires become tight during winter but sag a little during summer, because they are made of metal which _____________.
   (A) Expands on heating
   (B) Remains the same on heating
   (C) Contracts on heating
   (D) Changes shape on heating

7. Which of the following is not an example of the changes that occur by mixing two substances?
   (A) Salt dissolved in water
   (B) Mixing sand and water
   (C) Burning of a matchstick
   (D) Sugar dissolved in water

8. The changes which are not useful to us and may cause harm are called undesirable changes. Which of the following is/are example(s) of undesirable changes?
   (A) Eruption of volcano
   (B) Rusting of iron
   (C) Melting of ice
   (D) Both (A) and (B)

9. Which of the following are true?
   (A) Cooking rice is a physical change
   (B) Rotation of a fan is a fast change
   (C) Heat is absorbed or liberated during a change involving energy
   (D) (B) and (C) are true

10. Read the activity carefully.
    i.   Take two flasks, flask A and flask B.
    ii. In both of the flasks, take some lemon juice.
    iii. In flask A, add washing soda in the lemon juice.
    iv. In flask B, add salt in the lemon juice.

    Which could be the observation of this experiment?
    (A) Lots of bubbles will be formed in flask B because a chemical change takes place
    (B) Lots of bubbles will be formed in flask A because a chemical change takes place
    (C) Lots of bubbles will be formed in flask A because a physical change takes
    (D) Lots of bubbles will be observed in flask B because a physical change takes place

11. Physical changes can be generally reversed. Which of the following is an example of a physical change?
    i.   Zinc oxide, on heating, changes to yellow colour. However, on cooling, its colour changes to white.
    ii. When a piece of iron is stroked with a permanent magnet, it gets magnetized. However, if the magnetized iron is hammered, it loses its magnetism.
    iii. Wax, on being heated, changes into its liquid state. However, liquid wax changes into solid on cooling.
    (A) i and ii both   (B) Only iii
    (C) i, ii and iii   (D) None of these

12. Look at the following graph. It represents the energy consumption of a reaction. What kind of a change is it?

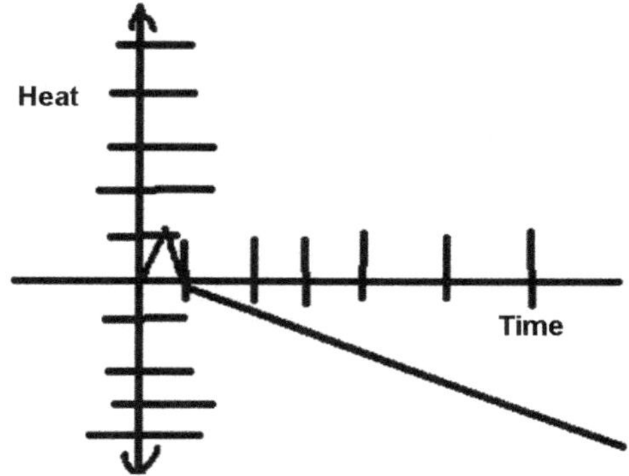

    (A) Physical change
    (B) Exothermic change
    (C) Endothermic change
    (D) Periodic change

13. Shahna took a small amount of lead nitrate in a dry test tube, holding the test tube with a test-tube holder. She put the test tube over the flame of the burner, and heated it. Soon a brown gas with a pungent smell is produced. The gas turns blue litmus red. She also observes a yellow solid residue remains in the test tube.

    Conclusion of the above experiment may be:
    (A) The brown gas evolved was nitrogen dioxide which is acidic in nature. The residue was yellow solid of lead oxide
    (B) The brown gas evolved was lead oxide which is acidic in nature. The residue was the yellow solid of nitrogen dioxide

(C) The brown gas evolved was acidic in nature. The residue was the yellow solid of nitrogen dioxide

(D) None of these

14. In which of the following statements is it proven that energy keeps on moving from one source to another and that it is not static?
   (A) Glowing of a light bulb
   (B) Burning of candle
   (C) Baking of cake
   (D) All of these

15. What property remains the same during physical or chemical changes?
   (A) Density
   (B) Shape
   (C) Mass
   (D) Arrangement of particles

16. Which of the following does not indicate a chemical change?
   (A) Change in colour
   (B) Change in shape
   (C) Change in energy
   (D) Change in odour

17. What is common among the following phenomena?
   i.   A slice of apple, if kept in the open, develops a brown colour.
   ii. Burning of magnesium ribbon.
   iii. A new substance is formed during this change.
   (A) All are examples of periodic changes
   (B) All are examples of undesirable changes
   (C) All are examples of chemical changes
   (D) All are examples of irreversible changes

18. Look at the flowchart and study it carefully.

P	Q
No new substance is formed during this change.	A new substance is formed during this change.
↓	↓
Composition of the substance does not change.	Composition of the substance changes.
↓	↓

Which of the following is correct?

(A) P: Reversible	Q: Irreversible
(B) P: Physical	Q: Chemical
(C) P: Reversible	Q: Reversible
(D) P: Chemical	Q: Physical

19. Which statement is not correct?
   (A) Rust is an iron compound which is formed due to the reaction between iron, water and oxygen
   (B) The reactions which are accompanied by release of heat are called exothermic reactions
   (C) When the temperature of a solid is increased, the thermal energy of its particles increases
   (D) When the temperature of a solid is increased, the kinetic energy of its particles increases

20. A teacher kept a beaker of water on a hot plate. The beaker is shown before and after the hot plate is turned on.

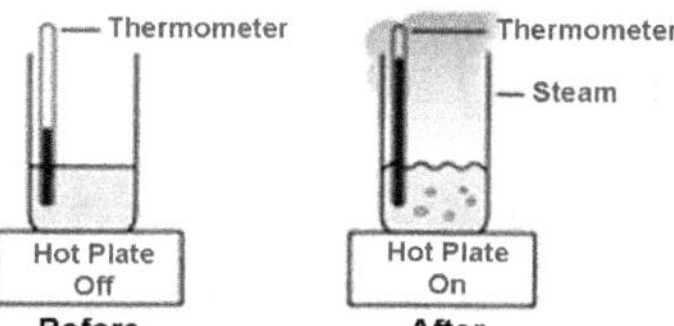

What evidence points to the fact that water is changing state?
(A) The hot plate is turned on
(B) The temperature increases
(C) The water bubbles and the steam is visible
(D) The mass of the water in the beaker increases

21. 10 gm of solid wax on melting will form _____ gm of molten wax.
(A) 20 gm   (B) 5 gm
(C) 10 gm   (D) 2.5 gm

22. Which of the following is an example of a periodic change?
(A) Landslide
(B) A car accident
(C) Heartbeat
(D) Eruption of volcano

23. A chunk of cement lying in the open gets wet due to rain during the night. The next day the sun shines brightly. What do you think happened to the cement? Could the change have been reversed?

(A) Due to the rainwater, the cement hardens and its composition changes. It is a chemical change and hence, cannot be reversed
(B) It is an irreversible change
(C) Yes, it is a reversible change
(D) Yes, it is a physical change and physical changes are usually reversible

24. If you pour a few drops of petrol on your palm, it will feel cool as the drops evaporate. This change is a/an _____.
(A) Chemical change
(B) Exothermic change
(C) Slow reaction
(D) Endothermic change

25. What are these examples of: the motion of planets around the sun, the motion of fans blades, and the blinking of traffic light?
(A) Undesirable changes
(B) Periodic changes
(C) Reversible change
(D) Chemical changes

26. In an endothermic reaction _____.
(A) Energy is not required
(B) Energy is absorbed
(C) Energy is neither released nor absorbed
(D) Energy is released

27. Medicines and food articles are labelled "store in a cool and dry place" to preserve them, because _____.
(A) Chemical reactions slow down in a cool environment
(B) Bacteria are frozen in a cool environment
(C) Microorganisms cannot survive in a cool environment
(D) Both (A) and (C)

28. The product formed by dissolving a substance into another is called _____.
(A) A compound   (B) A solution
(C) A solvent   (D) A solute

29. Atoms combine through the _____.
(A) Rise in temperature
(B) Interaction of protons
(C) Interaction of electrons
(D) Presence of a catalyst

30. Substances react with each other and form chemical bonds to _____.
(A) Form newer compounds
(B) Increase their energy
(C) Decrease their energy
(D) Become stable compounds

31. Which of the following statement(s) is true for formation of compost from vegetable waste:
    i. It is a physical change.
    ii. An irreversible change and a slow change.
    iii. A chemical and non-desirable change.
    iv. A chemical and desirable change.
    (A) i and ii
    (B) ii and iii
    (C) iii and iv
    (D) iv only

32. If bread is baked, the observational changes which support it being a chemical change are:
    i. Change in odour
    ii. Change in texture
    iii. Change in taste
    iv. Bread remains bread
    (A) i only
    (B) i and ii only
    (C) i, ii and iii
    (D) iv only

33. Which of the following are desirable changes?
    (i) Drying of clothes
    (ii) Growth of weeds
    (iii) Cement getting hard when exposed to moisture
    (iv) Desalination of sea water
    (A) Only (i) and (ii)
    (B) Only (ii) and (iii)
    (C) Only (i) and (iv)
    (D) Only (i), (ii) and (iv)

34. What is the change taking place in the following processes?

$$Ice \underset{cooling}{\overset{heating}{\rightleftharpoons}} Water \underset{cooling}{\overset{heating}{\rightleftharpoons}} Steam$$

    (A) Irreversible, physical change
    (B) Chemical change
    (C) Reversible, physical change
    (D) Reversible, chemical change

35. Nitu mixed some iron filings with sulphur powder in a China dish. She heated the contents of China dish. What did she observe during the experiment?
    (A) There was no difference in the contents of China dish before and after heating.
    (B) Before heating, iron filings and sulphur powder could be seen separately but after heating the content became black.
    (C) Before heating, the iron filings and sulphur powder could not be seen separately.
    (D) Before heating, the contents were black and after heating, iron filings and sulphur could be seen separately.

Darken Your Choice with HB Pencil

1.	Ⓐ Ⓑ Ⓒ Ⓓ	8.	Ⓐ Ⓑ Ⓒ Ⓓ	15.	Ⓐ Ⓑ Ⓒ Ⓓ	22	Ⓐ Ⓑ Ⓒ Ⓓ	29.	Ⓐ Ⓑ Ⓒ Ⓓ
2.	Ⓐ Ⓑ Ⓒ Ⓓ	9.	Ⓐ Ⓑ Ⓒ Ⓓ	16.	Ⓐ Ⓑ Ⓒ Ⓓ	23.	Ⓐ Ⓑ Ⓒ Ⓓ	30.	Ⓐ Ⓑ Ⓒ Ⓓ
3.	Ⓐ Ⓑ Ⓒ Ⓓ	10.	Ⓐ Ⓑ Ⓒ Ⓓ	17.	Ⓐ Ⓑ Ⓒ Ⓓ	24.	Ⓐ Ⓑ Ⓒ Ⓓ	31.	Ⓐ Ⓑ Ⓒ Ⓓ
4.	Ⓐ Ⓑ Ⓒ Ⓓ	11.	Ⓐ Ⓑ Ⓒ Ⓓ	18.	Ⓐ Ⓑ Ⓒ Ⓓ	25.	Ⓐ Ⓑ Ⓒ Ⓓ	32.	Ⓐ Ⓑ Ⓒ Ⓓ
5.	Ⓐ Ⓑ Ⓒ Ⓓ	12.	Ⓐ Ⓑ Ⓒ Ⓓ	19.	Ⓐ Ⓑ Ⓒ Ⓓ	26.	Ⓐ Ⓑ Ⓒ Ⓓ	33.	Ⓐ Ⓑ Ⓒ Ⓓ
6.	Ⓐ Ⓑ Ⓒ Ⓓ	13.	Ⓐ Ⓑ Ⓒ Ⓓ	20.	Ⓐ Ⓑ Ⓒ Ⓓ	27.	Ⓐ Ⓑ Ⓒ Ⓓ	34.	Ⓐ Ⓑ Ⓒ Ⓓ
7.	Ⓐ Ⓑ Ⓒ Ⓓ	14.	Ⓐ Ⓑ Ⓒ Ⓓ	21.	Ⓐ Ⓑ Ⓒ Ⓓ	28.	Ⓐ Ⓑ Ⓒ Ⓓ	35.	Ⓐ Ⓑ Ⓒ Ⓓ

LEARNING OBJECTIVES

➤ Characteristics of living and non-living things
➤ Differences between living and non-living things
➤ Organisms and their surroundings

MULTIPLE CHOICE QUESTIONS

1. Which among these children made a correct statement?
   (A) Saumya: Global warming increases the concentration of carbon dioxide in the atmosphere
   (B) Sumit: Global warming increases the concentration of nitrogen in the atmosphere
   (C) Sanchit: Global warming increases the concentration of oxygen in the atmosphere
   (D) Ashi: Global warming increases the concentration of ozone in the atmosphere

2. Which of the following characteristics of a glass of water reason that it cannot be considered alive?
   (A) It has no heart
   (B) It has no arms or legs
   (C) It has no cells
   (D) It has no tissues

3. Some yeast, sugar and water are mixed in a test-tube. The diagrams show the test-tube at the start and after one hour.

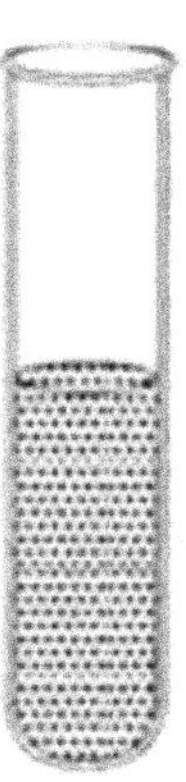 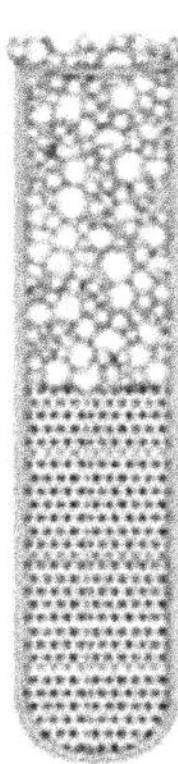

   Which process causes this change?
   (A) Growth   (B) Irritability
   (C) Reproduction   (D) Respiration

4. Excretion, irritability and reproduction are characteristics of ____________.
   (A) All animals and plants
   (B) Animals only
   (C) Plants only
   (D) All animals and some plants only

5. Look at the following picture carefully. Which of the following characteristic of living organisms is it showing?

Venus Flytrap

(A) Living things are made of cells
(B) Living things obtain and use energy
(C) Living things grow and develop
(D) Living things require food for energy

6. One of the characteristics of living organisms is that they all respire by __________.

(A) Obtaining oxygen by breathing
(B) Obtaining energy from sunlight
(C) Obtaining energy by chemically breaking down food
(D) Breaking down large molecules to smaller molecules by digestion

7. The following picture is an example of __________ in plants. The picture is of __________.

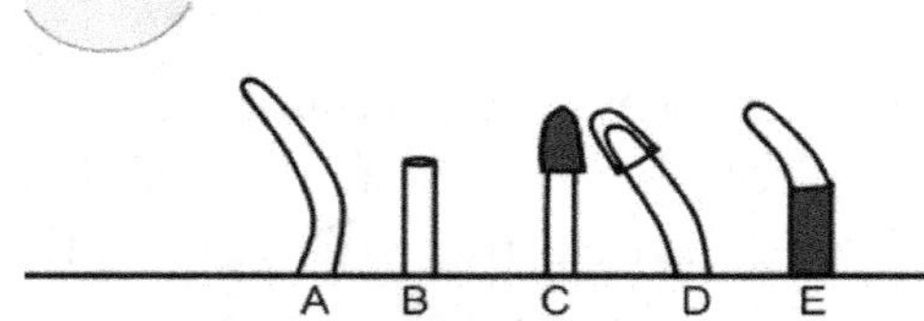

(A) Sensitivity, germination of seeds
(B) Locomotion, seed dispersal
(C) Locomotion, wilting
(D) Sensitivity, phototropism

8. Which of the following organisms is not ultimately dependent on the sun as a source of energy?
(A) A night-blooming flower is pollinated by night-flying bats
(B) An underground earthworm avoids the sun

(C) A cave fish feeds on debris that washes down to it
(D) No, all the organisms are ultimately dependent on the sun

9. What is the term which refers to all the chemical energy transformations that occur within a cell?
(A) Evolution   (B) Metabolism
(C) Adaptation   (D) Homeostasis

10. Soham set up two small aquariums at home. He placed three rainbow fish in each aquarium but he put hydrilla plants in aquarium A only. After some time he observed that that the fish swam freely in aquarium A but the fish in aquarium B swam near the water surface.

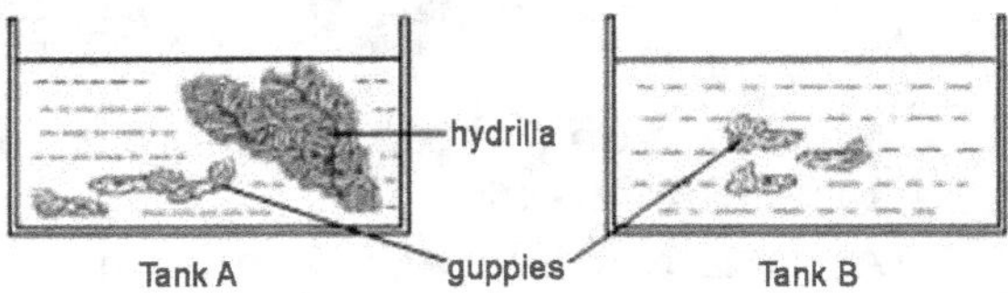

He concluded that the hydrilla plants __________.

(A) Help to beautify the aquarium
(B) Provide shade for the fish
(C) Provide oxygen for the fish to breathe during photosynthesis
(D) Are the main source of food for the fish

11. Study the diagram as shown below.

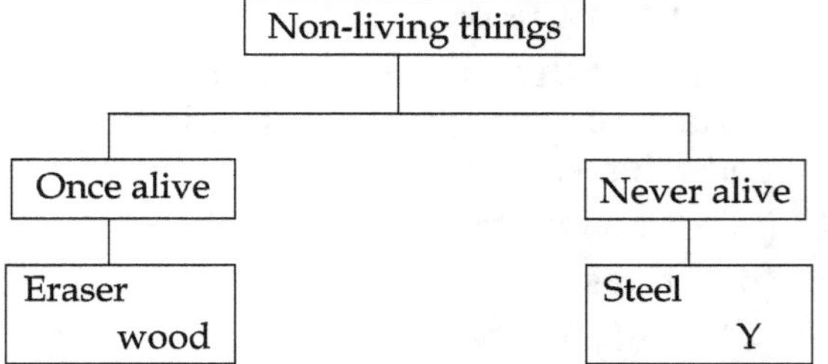

Which one of the following is an example of Y?
(A) Glass bottle
(B) Cotton shirt
(C) Exercise book
(D) Dried flower

12. Study the diagram below:

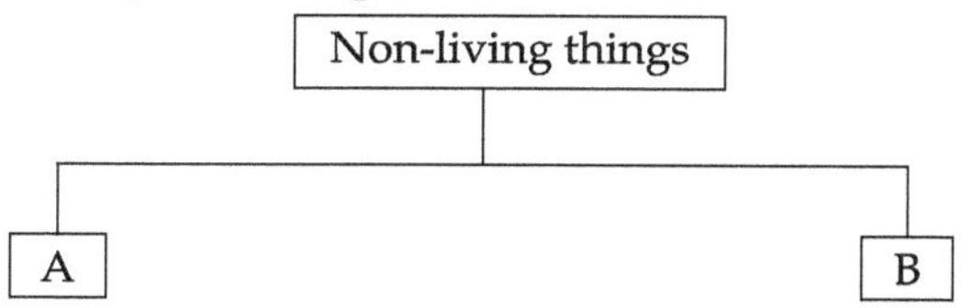

Which group of items can you put into box A?

(A) Glass bottle, paper clip, cotton shirt
(B) Paper plate, plastic fork and spoon
(C) Leather sofa, rubber boots, bamboo cane
(D) Rubber balls, plastic cup, metal spoon

13. John set up two tanks. He placed three guppies in each tank but he put hydrilla plants in Tank A only. John found that the fish swam freely in Tank A but the fish in Tank B swam near the water surface.

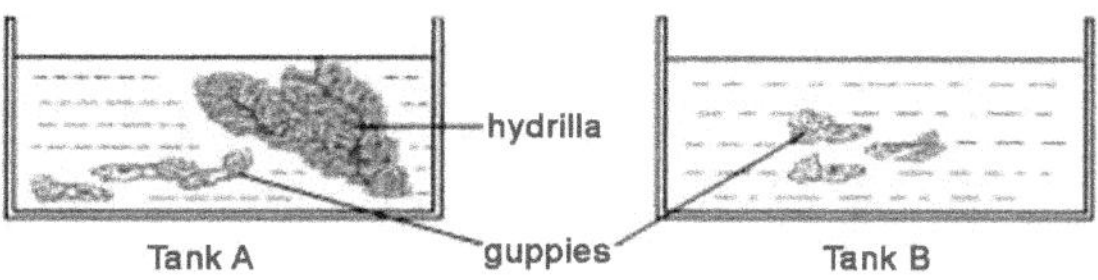

In the night, both the guppies and the hydrilla plants take in _______ and give out _______.

(A) Oxygen; oxygen
(B) Carbon dioxide; oxygen
(C) Oxygen; carbon dioxide
(D) Carbon dioxide; carbon dioxide

14. Some green beans were placed on some damp cotton wool in a dish and placed in a dark corner. A few days later, the beans started to grow into seedlings. The beans get their food for growth from the _______.

(A) Air
(B) Cotton wool
(C) Seed-leaves
(D) Water used to damp the cotton wool

15. Which of the following describes respiration?

Ananya: Animals take in carbon dioxide and give off oxygen.

Sanchit: Animals take in oxygen and give off carbon dioxide.

Saumya: Plants take in carbon dioxide and give off oxygen.

Ranchit: Plants take in oxygen and give off carbon dioxide.

(A) Ananya and Ranchit
(B) Sanchit and Saumya
(C) Sanchit and Ranchit
(D) Ranchit only

16. Animals have structural and behavioural adaptations which enable them to survive in their natural habitats.

By looking at the picture of the head of the fish, which of the following is true of how this organism survives in its natural habitat?

(A) It is a herbivore
(B) It has sharp teeth to feed on other animals
(C) It uses its eyes to scare away predators
(D) It is able to hold its breath underwater for a long time

17. The following aquatic animals are grouped according to their breathing adaptations. Which group of animals does not breathe in the same way?

(A) Water stick insect, water scorpion
(B) Tubifex worm, tadpole
(C) Crab, wood louse
(D) Water spider, great diving beetle`

18. Which of the following animals have the correct form of adaptation?
    (A) Camel: bristles on his feet
    (B) Whale: blow holes in its head
    (C) Mudskipper: lungs for breathing
    (D) Birds: compact bones

19. Animals use different parts of their bodies to move around.

    In the following table, the body parts used by the corresponding animals are matched. Which animal is matched incorrectly?

Animal	Legs	Wings	Fins	Flippers	Body
Snake					Y
Penguin		Y			
Cheetah	Y				
Dolphin			Y	Y	

    (A) Snake   (B) Penguin
    (C) Cheetah   (D) Dolphin

20. Based on the diagrams of the dolphin and the fish (not drawn to scale), which characteristic they share in common?

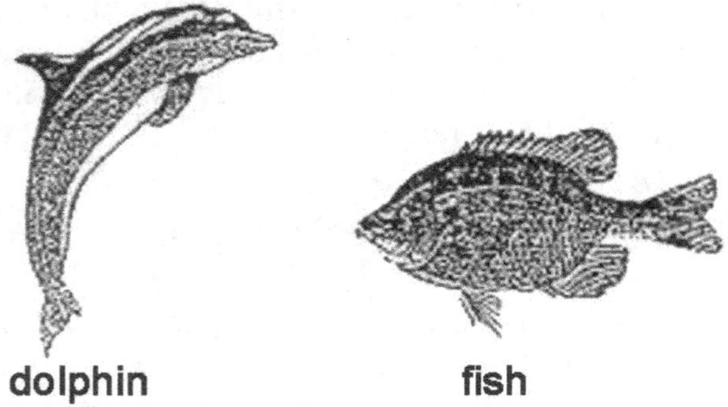

    i.   They both have whiskers.
    ii. Each has a tail to propel itself forward in the water.
    iii. Both have gills to breath.
    iv. Both are warm blooded.
    (A) Only ii
    (B) i and iv only
    (C) ii and iii only
    (D) iii and iv only

21. Mike had a glass tank containing some earthworms, dead leaves and maize seeds. He added another animal into the tank. He observed the tank for a few hours. Then he drew a graph to show his observations.

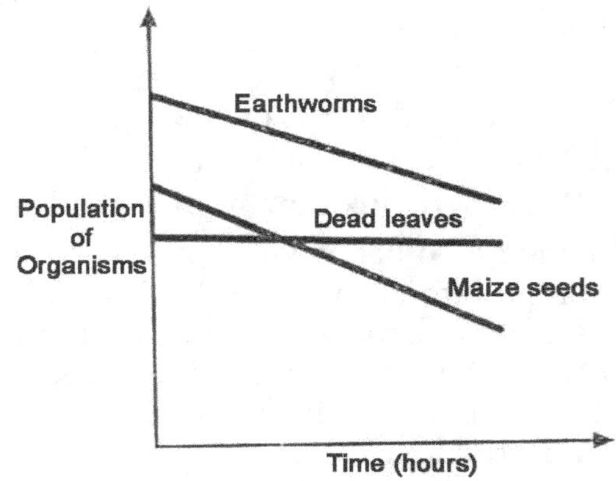

    By looking at the graph, we can tell that the animal that Mike put in was a __________.

    (A) Snail   (B) Chick
    (C) Toad   (D) Grasshopper

22. Samantha found a healthy plant with red leaves in her garden. She said that the plant is not able to make food because its leaves are not green. Is Samantha correct?

(A) Yes. The plant does not have green leaves. Hence, it will not make its own food but gets its food from the ground

(B) Yes. The plant does not have green leaves. Hence, it does not have chlorophyll to absorb sunlight to make food

(C) No. Even though the plant has no green leaves, it can still make food through its underground stem

(D) No. The green pigment, chlorophyll, is hidden under the red pigment in the leaves. Hence, the plant can still make food

23. Study the flowchart below carefully.

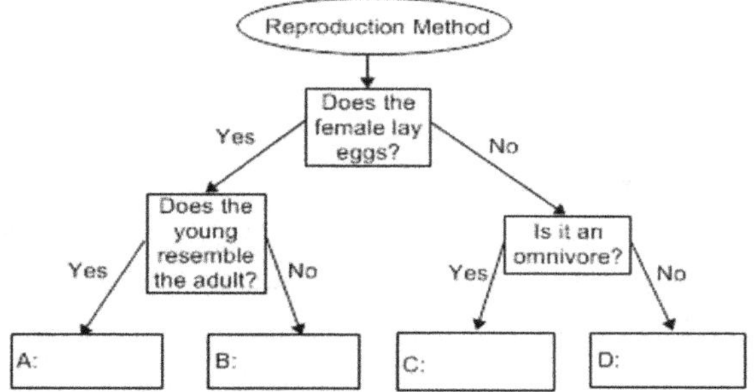

Put the following animals: lizard, zebra, man and dragonfly on the boxes above.

(A) A: Lizard; B: Dragonfly; C: Man; D: Zebra

(B) A: Zebra; B: Dragonfly; C: Man; D: Lizard

(C) A: Dragonfly; B: Dragonfly; C: Man; D: Lizard

(D) A: Man; B: Dragonfly; C: Lizard; D: Zebra

24. Based on the information below, answer the following questions:

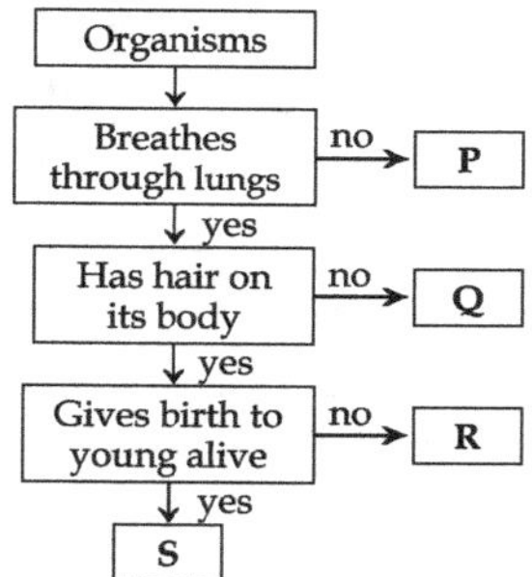

Identify the characteristic(s) that is/are common for both organisms R and S.

(A) They breathe through gills and have hair on their body

(B) They breathe through lungs and have hair on their body

(C) They breathe through nose and have hair on their body

(D) They breathe through lungs

25. Look at the following pictures carefully.

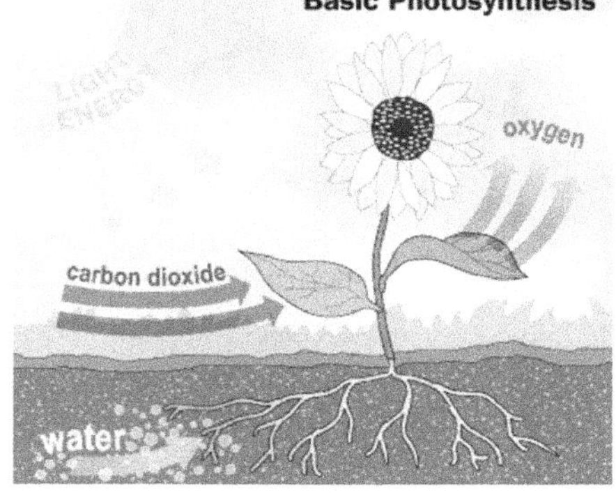

The two living organisms in these pictures are __________ and the common life process that occurs in both the living organism is.

(A) Plant and mushroom, respiration
(B) Plant and animal, photosynthesis
(C) Plant and snail, mobility
(D) Plant and snail, excretion

26. Which living organisms excrete uric acid?
(A) Birds and lizards
(B) Birds and reptiles
(C) Birds
(D) Both (A) and (B)

27. When plants grow in dark, they become tall, yellowish and weak, and the leaves are very small.

This happens because of __________.
(A) Lack of sunlight
(B) Lack of photosynthesis
(C) Lack of photosynthesis due to no sunlight
(D) Lack of air

28. Read the features of a plant as given below:
i. They have waxy upper surface.
ii. Leaves are large and flat.
iii. Roots are much reduced in size.
iv. Stems are generally long and narrow.

To which of the following habitats does this plant belong?

(A) Polar region
(B) Desert
(C) Aquatic
(D) Tropical rainforest

29. What is a common character among the following animals?

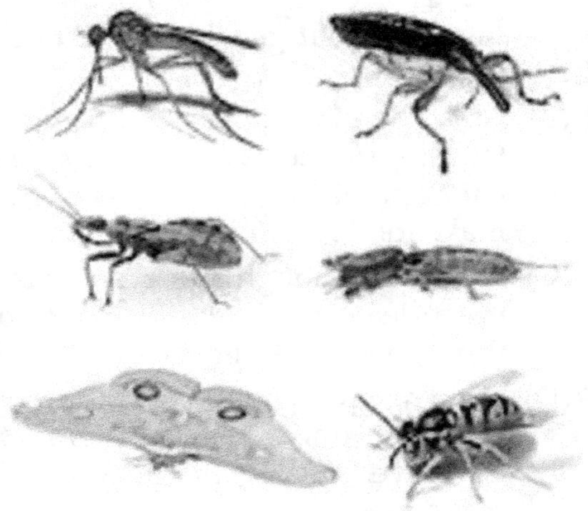

(A) They all lack backbone
(B) They all live in water
(C) They all lay eggs to reproduce
(D) They all have scales on their body

30. Four groups of mice were taken for an experiment. One group was control group and other three were test groups. The test groups consume different amounts of sweetener in their food. The control group is the one that receives __________.

(A) 10 mg/day of sweetener
(B) 50 mg/day of sweetener
(C) No sweetener
(D) Extra food

Read the following paragraph and answer the questions that follow.

Shobhit performed the following activities at home. He soaked green gram (moong) seeds in water overnight in a bowl. Next morning, he drained out the excess water and kept the wet seeds in the folds of a muslin cloth. (We should keep the cloth moist all the time by sprinkling the water at regular intervals [once or twice every day]). After another 24 hours, he checked them again. He saw that the seeds began to sprout.

31. Choose the correct option and answer the following questions.
    I. Which part of the plant is used in the previous activity?
    II. What makes the nutrient contents increase in the seeds?

	I	II
(A)	Seeds	Germination
(B)	Grains	Germination
(C)	Seeds	Sprouting
(D)	Seeds	Soaking

32. The following flow-chart shows the classification of micro-organisms.

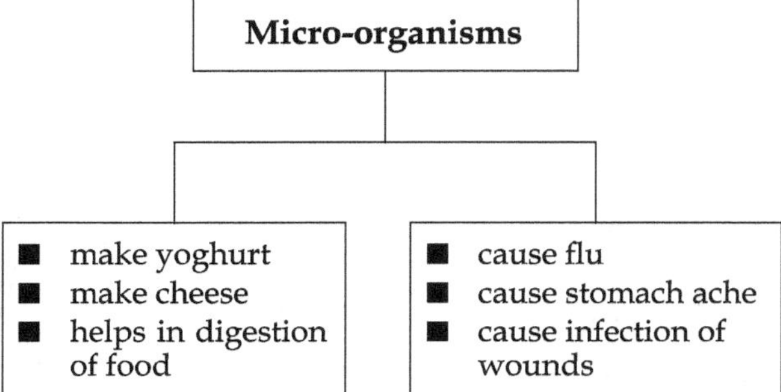

Based on the above information, explain the uses of micro-organisms grouped.
    i. Whether they are useful to man
    ii. Whether they reproduce from spores
    iii. According to the number of cells (single-celled or multi-celled)
(A) i only
(B) ii only
(C) i and ii only
(D) ii and iii only

33. The diagrams below show the life-cycle of organisms X and Y.

Organism X	Organism Y

On the basis of the diagrams, which of the following statement(s) is/are true?
    i. Both the adults of organisms X and Y are able to fly.
    ii. The young of organism X does not look like its adult while the young of organism Y looks like its adult.
    iii. Organism X has a 4-stage life cycle while organism Y has a 3-stage life cycle.
(A) iii only
(B) i and ii only
(C) ii and iii only
(D) i, ii and iii

34. Which option is not an adaptation of animals living in polar regions?

   (A) Wide and large paws.

   (B) Layer of fat under skin.

   (C) Thin skin with scales

   (D) Strong sense of smell

35. Which of the following statement(s) is/are correct?

   (A) Xerophytes refers to desert plants and animals.

   (B) There are no roots in desert plants.

   (C) Desert plants do not show the process of transpiration.

   (D) In mountains regions we see different kinds of adaptations at different heights.

1.	Ⓐ Ⓑ Ⓒ Ⓓ	8.	Ⓐ Ⓑ Ⓒ Ⓓ	15.	Ⓐ Ⓑ Ⓒ Ⓓ	22	Ⓐ Ⓑ Ⓒ Ⓓ	29.	Ⓐ Ⓑ Ⓒ Ⓓ
2.	Ⓐ Ⓑ Ⓒ Ⓓ	9.	Ⓐ Ⓑ Ⓒ Ⓓ	16.	Ⓐ Ⓑ Ⓒ Ⓓ	23.	Ⓐ Ⓑ Ⓒ Ⓓ	30.	Ⓐ Ⓑ Ⓒ Ⓓ
3.	Ⓐ Ⓑ Ⓒ Ⓓ	10.	Ⓐ Ⓑ Ⓒ Ⓓ	17.	Ⓐ Ⓑ Ⓒ Ⓓ	24.	Ⓐ Ⓑ Ⓒ Ⓓ	31.	Ⓐ Ⓑ Ⓒ Ⓓ
4.	Ⓐ Ⓑ Ⓒ Ⓓ	11.	Ⓐ Ⓑ Ⓒ Ⓓ	18.	Ⓐ Ⓑ Ⓒ Ⓓ	25.	Ⓐ Ⓑ Ⓒ Ⓓ	32.	Ⓐ Ⓑ Ⓒ Ⓓ
5.	Ⓐ Ⓑ Ⓒ Ⓓ	12.	Ⓐ Ⓑ Ⓒ Ⓓ	19.	Ⓐ Ⓑ Ⓒ Ⓓ	26.	Ⓐ Ⓑ Ⓒ Ⓓ	33.	Ⓐ Ⓑ Ⓒ Ⓓ
6.	Ⓐ Ⓑ Ⓒ Ⓓ	13.	Ⓐ Ⓑ Ⓒ Ⓓ	20.	Ⓐ Ⓑ Ⓒ Ⓓ	27.	Ⓐ Ⓑ Ⓒ Ⓓ	34.	Ⓐ Ⓑ Ⓒ Ⓓ
7.	Ⓐ Ⓑ Ⓒ Ⓓ	14.	Ⓐ Ⓑ Ⓒ Ⓓ	21.	Ⓐ Ⓑ Ⓒ Ⓓ	28.	Ⓐ Ⓑ Ⓒ Ⓓ	35.	Ⓐ Ⓑ Ⓒ Ⓓ

MOTION AND MEASUREMENT OF DISTANCES

LEARNING OBJECTIVES

➤ The science behind motion and its different types
➤ Measuring distances

MULTIPLE CHOICE QUESTIONS

1. Movement of a branch of a tree in air is an example of __________.
   (A) Random motion
   (B) Circular motion
   (C) Periodic motion
   (D) Rotational motion

2. Which of the following statements is correct?
   (A) A footstep can be used as a standard unit of measurement because its length is same for all the people.
   (B) A footstep cannot be used as a standard unit of measurement because its length is not same for all the people.
   (C) A footstep cannot be used as a standard unit of measurement because its length is 10 cm only for all the people.
   (D) A footstep cannot be used as a standard unit of measurement because it always remains constant.

3. Who found that a pendulum of a given length always takes the same time to complete one oscillation?
   (A) Galileo Galilei   (B) Archimedes
   (C) Albert Einstein   (D) Newton

4. The scale should be kept __________ the length while measuring a length.
   (A) Perpendicular to
   (B) Inclined to
   (C) Away from
   (D) Along

5. When the bob of the pendulum is released after taking it slightly to one side, it:
   (A) Begins to move up and down
   (B) Begins to move to and fro
   (C) Becomes still and does not move
   (D) Comes to rest at the mean position

6. The motion of a rolling ball is an example of __________ motion.
   (A) Circular   (B) Linear
   (C) Rotational   (D) Random

7. Identify the types of motion from the images below.

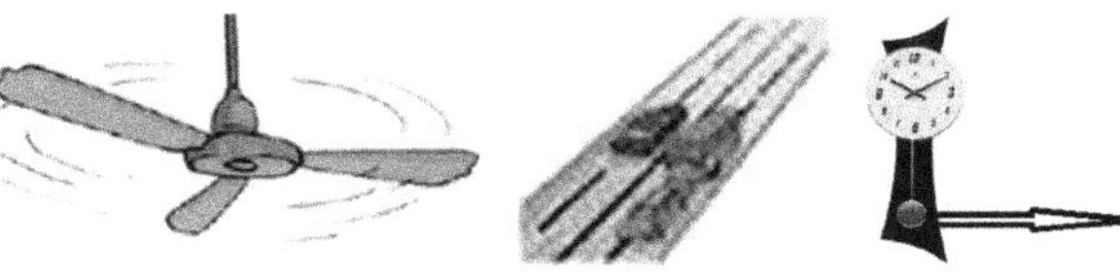

   (A) Periodic, rotational, linear respectively
   (B) Periodic, rotational, circular respectively

(C) Linear, rotational, periodic respectively

(D) Rotational, linear, periodic respectively

8. Three cars are running on the road with three different speeds: 78 mph, 59 mph, and 65 mph respectively. Calculate the average of these three speeds.

(A) 82.7 mph   (B) 74.5 mph

(C) 67.3 mph   (D) 44.2 mph

9. What would be the best unit to use to measure the tip of your pencil?

(A) Feet   (B) Kilometer

(C) Millimeter   (D) Meter

10. Look at the following picture carefully.

Now read the following paragraph carefully and fill the blank with correct sequence of words.

A stone suspended with a non-stretchable thread makes a simple __________. When the pendulum is at rest, it is at position B. This is called the rest position or its __________. When it swings, it moves from B to A, back to B, from B to C and back to B. This completes one full swing of the pendulum. Each swing is called __________.

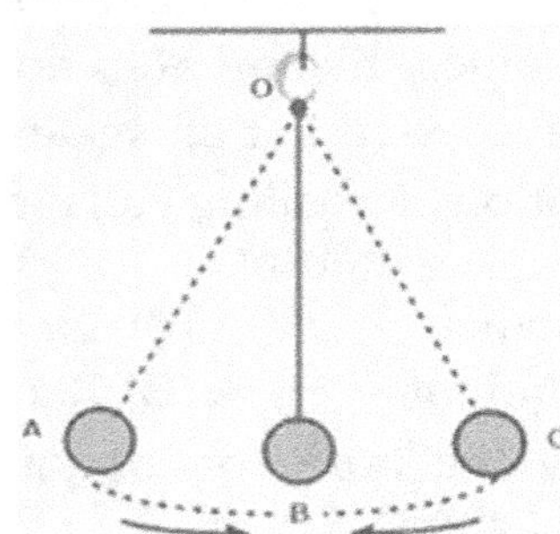

(A) Mean position, one oscillation, pendulum

(B) One oscillation, complete oscillation, pendulum

(C) Mean position, pendulum, complete oscillation

(D) Pendulum, mean position, one oscillation

11. Two athletes take part in two separate races and cover different distances in different times. Kavya runs 2 km in 10 minutes and Yamini runs 5 km in 20 minutes on two different tracks. Which of the following statements is correct?

(A) Yamini runs faster than Kavya

(B) Kavya runs faster than Yamini

(C) Yamini runs faster than Kavya in one minute

(D) Both (A) and (C)

12. Which of the following is a unit of speed?

(A) km/min   (B) m/min

(C) km/h   (D) kg/s

13. Look at the picture carefully: Fill in the blanks using words: stationary, moving.

The potter at the railway station is __________ in relation to the train, but is __________ in relation to the bag on his head.

(A) Moving, stationary

(B) Stationary, moving

(C) Stationary, stationary

(D) Moving, moving

14. Why is measurement important to us?

(A) It is required by students to learn mathematics and science

(B) It is required only for advanced scientific calculations

(C) It is required by every human being for their day-to-day living

(D) It is required only to build satellites

15. Read the following two paragraphs. Analyze the situation and choose the correct options.

1. A bus runs from Kolkata to Guwahati. It covers a distance of 400 km in 7 hours and then a distance of 550 km in the next 7 hours.

2. Alisha takes part in a car race. She drives a distance of 70 km each in the first, second and third hours.

(A) First statement is an example of uniform motion and second statement is an example of non-uniform motion

(B) First statement is an example of non-uniform motion and second statement is an example of uniform motion

(C) Both first and second are examples of uniform motion

(D) Both first and second are examples of non-uniform motion

16. 1 cm = ………. m
(A) 0.001　　(B) 0.01
(C) 10　　(D) 0.1

17. The length of the blank card shown below is ____________.

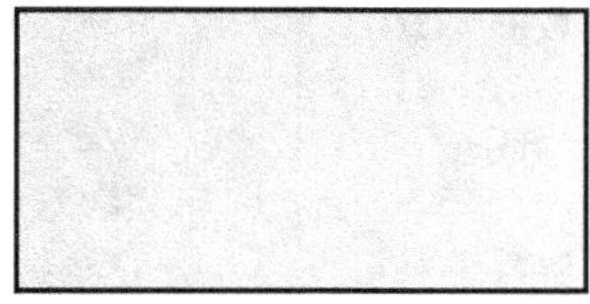

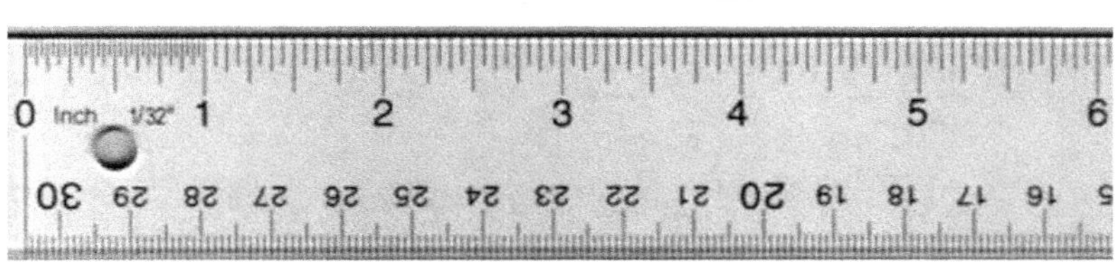

(A) 1.6 inches　　(B) 1.6 cm　　(C) 3.2 cm　　(D) 2.5 inches

18. Which of the following objects cannot be used for measuring the length of a curved line?
(A) Thread and ruler
(B) Screw gauge
(C) Set square
(D) None of them

19. While reading an instrument, why is it important to place the eye in line with the reading?
(A) To avoid parallax error
(B) To see more clearly
(C) To avoid reflections
(D) To get a better view of the entire instrument

20. Look at the following graph. Observe it carefully.

This graph shows:

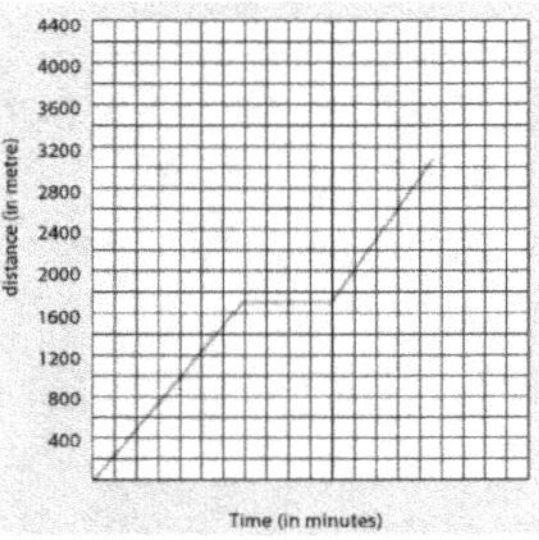

(A) The motion of a school bus
(B) The motion of Sanchit, who stops at the market on his way back home from school
(C) The motion of an ant as it collects rice grains
(D) The motion of an athlete running a 200 m race

21. A cyclist moves from a certain point X and goes round a circle of radius 'a' and

reaches Y, exactly at the other side of the point X as shown in the figure below. The displacement of the cyclist would be __________.

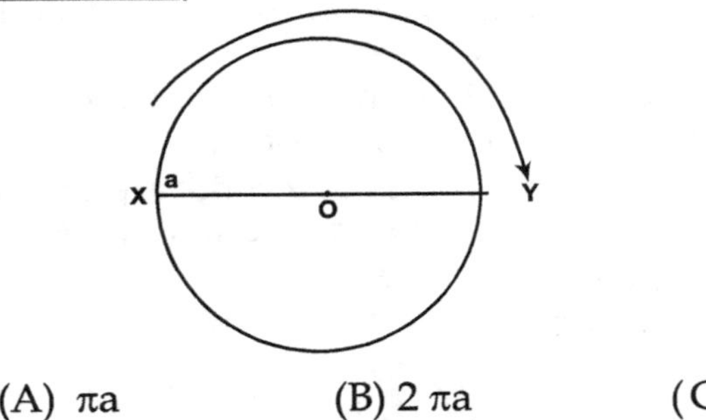

(A) πa (B) 2 πa (C) 2a
(D) 2 π/a

22. The unit of speed depends on the units of distance and time. Based on this statement, fill up the following table.

Units for distance	Units for time	Units for speed	
kilometers		kilometers per hour	Km/h
	second		
meter	minute		m/ min

(A) Hour, meter, meters per second, m/sec, meter/minute
(B) Second, meter/minute, meter/second, m/sec
(C) Meter, meter/second, meter/minute, m/sec,
(D) Meter/minute, centimeter, minute, Km/h

23. In circular motion, the __________.
(A) Acceleration is zero
(B) Velocity is constant
(C) Direction of the motion fixed
(D) Direction of the motion changes continuously

24. Which of the following is false?
(A) A ceiling fan shows rotatory motion
(B) The motion of a swing is rectilinear as well as circular
(C) A guitar shows vibratory motion
(D) The pendulum of a clock shows oscillatory motion

25. The picture here shows the position of the sun at different times of the day, if we were looking south. The picture also shows the shadow cast by the stick at 4 p.m.

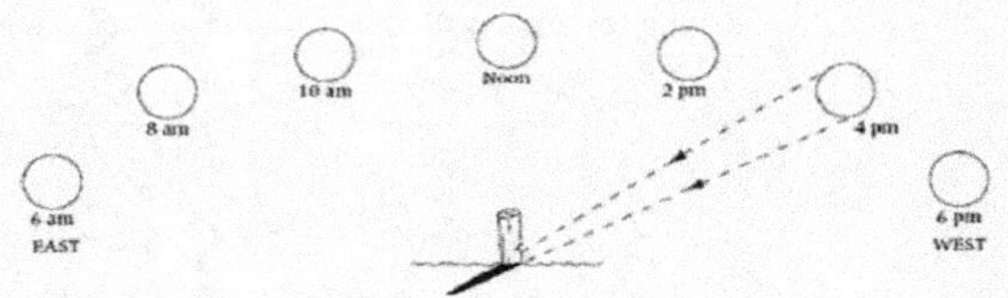

What time of the day would it be if the stick made shadows like these?

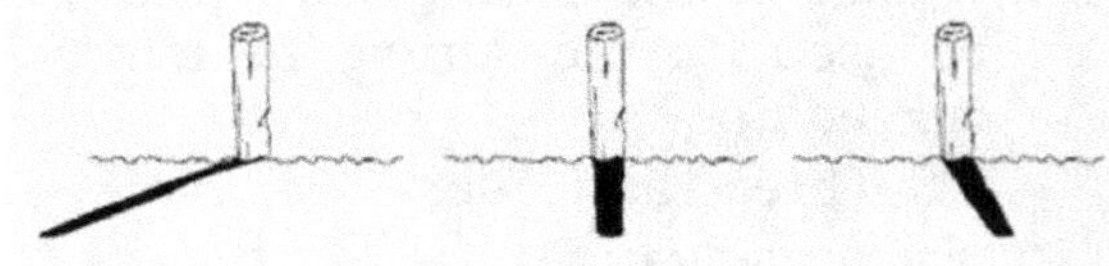

(A) 6 pm, noon, 8 am
(B) 10 am, noon, 4 pm
(C) 6 pm, noon, 10 am
(D) 8 am, noon, 6 pm

HOTS (ACHIEVERS SECTION)

26. Match column I with column II and choose the correct option:

Column I	Column II
a. Metre	i. Non-standard unit of length
b. Yard	ii. Unit to measure small distance
c. Millimetre	iii. S.I. Unit of length
d. Hand span	iv. Unit to measure long distances

e. Kilometre   v. Standard unit of length

(A) a-iv, b-v, c-ii, d-i, e-iii
(B) a-iii, b-v, c-ii, d-i, e-iv
(C) a-iv, b-ii, c-v, d-i, e-iii
(D) a-iv, b-i, c-v, d-ii, e-iii

27. Column I defines the kind of activity and column II defines the type of motion. Match column I with column II and choose the correct option.

Column I	Column II
1. Motion of a potter wheel	o. Random motion
2. A falling stone	p. Vibratory motion
3. A spinning top	q. Rectilinear motion
4. Motion of mosquito in flight	r. Circular motion
5. Plucking the string of a guitar	s. Rotatory motion

(A) 1-s, 2-q, 3-r, 4-o, 5-p
(B) 1-r, 2-q, 3-s, 4-o, 5-p
(C) 1-q, 2-p, 3-r, 4-o, 5-s
(D) 1-s, 2-o, 3-r, 4-q, 5-p

28. Which type of motion is represented by the plastic ruler shown below?

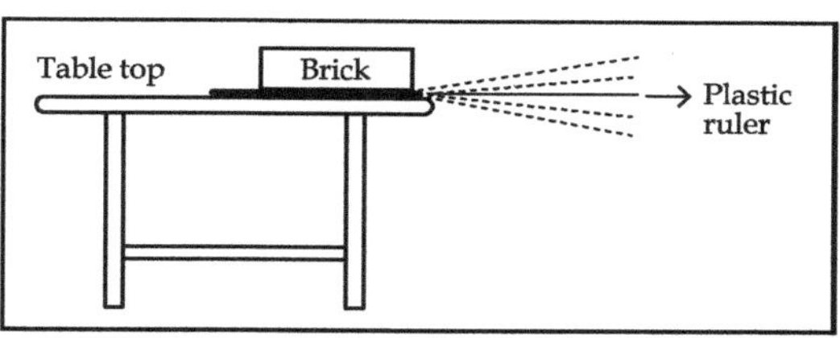

(A) Circular   (B) Translatory
(C) Rotatory   (D) Vibratory

29. Identify the motion of the block shown in the figure.

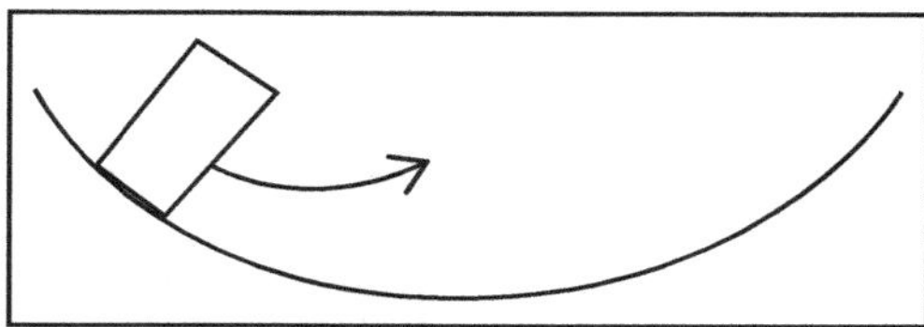

(A) Oscillatory motion
(B) Translatory motion
(C) Curvilinear motion
(D) Periodic motion

30. Which of the given figures show periodic motion?

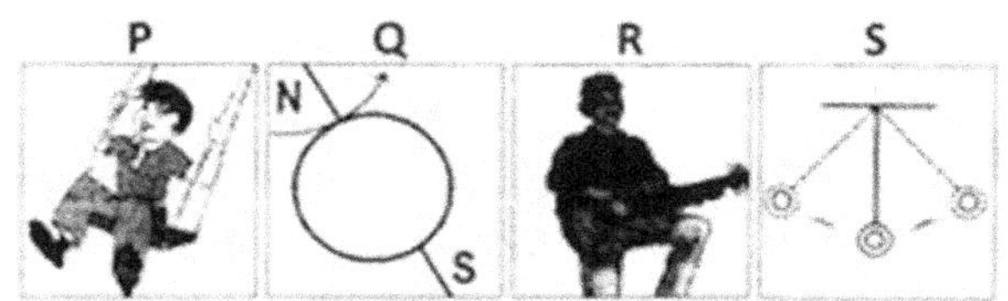

(A) Q and S   (B) P and Q
(C) Q and R   (D) R and S

1.	Ⓐ Ⓑ Ⓒ Ⓓ	7.	Ⓐ Ⓑ Ⓒ Ⓓ	13.	Ⓐ Ⓑ Ⓒ Ⓓ	19	Ⓐ Ⓑ Ⓒ Ⓓ	25.	Ⓐ Ⓑ Ⓒ Ⓓ
2.	Ⓐ Ⓑ Ⓒ Ⓓ	8.	Ⓐ Ⓑ Ⓒ Ⓓ	14.	Ⓐ Ⓑ Ⓒ Ⓓ	20.	Ⓐ Ⓑ Ⓒ Ⓓ	26.	Ⓐ Ⓑ Ⓒ Ⓓ
3.	Ⓐ Ⓑ Ⓒ Ⓓ	9.	Ⓐ Ⓑ Ⓒ Ⓓ	15.	Ⓐ Ⓑ Ⓒ Ⓓ	21.	Ⓐ Ⓑ Ⓒ Ⓓ	27.	Ⓐ Ⓑ Ⓒ Ⓓ
4.	Ⓐ Ⓑ Ⓒ Ⓓ	10.	Ⓐ Ⓑ Ⓒ Ⓓ	16.	Ⓐ Ⓑ Ⓒ Ⓓ	22.	Ⓐ Ⓑ Ⓒ Ⓓ	28.	Ⓐ Ⓑ Ⓒ Ⓓ
5.	Ⓐ Ⓑ Ⓒ Ⓓ	11.	Ⓐ Ⓑ Ⓒ Ⓓ	17.	Ⓐ Ⓑ Ⓒ Ⓓ	23.	Ⓐ Ⓑ Ⓒ Ⓓ	29.	Ⓐ Ⓑ Ⓒ Ⓓ
6.	Ⓐ Ⓑ Ⓒ Ⓓ	12.	Ⓐ Ⓑ Ⓒ Ⓓ	18.	Ⓐ Ⓑ Ⓒ Ⓓ	24.	Ⓐ Ⓑ Ⓒ Ⓓ	30.	Ⓐ Ⓑ Ⓒ Ⓓ

LIGHT, SHADOWS AND REFLECTION

LEARNING OBJECTIVES

➤ Important characteristics of light
➤ Luminous and non-luminous objects
➤ Opaque, transparent and translucent objects

MULTIPLE CHOICE QUESTIONS

1. Why do the shadows made by the sun change in size during the course of the day?
   (A) Because the weather changes
   (B) Because the objects keep moving
   (C) Because the sun appears to move across the sky during the course of the day
   (D) Because the amount of light, emitted by the sun, keeps on changing

2. Light is a form of energy that is produced by a:
   (A) Transparent object
   (B) Luminous object
   (C) Non-luminous object
   (D) Opaque object

3. If a capital letter R is seen in an ordinary plane mirror, what does it look like?
   (A) R   (B) Я
   (C) Я   (D) Я

4. The image of an object formed in the water is:
   (A) Diminished
   (B) Erect
   (C) Inverted
   (D) None of these

5. Ishani saw the sun at different positions in the sky at different times of the day. Which one of the following is the cause for her observations?
   (A) Revolution of the earth
   (B) Rotation of the sun
   (C) Rotation of the earth
   (D) Movement of the earth around the moon

6. Which of the following will not form a circular shadow?
   (A) A CD
   (B) Shoe box
   (C) Ice-cream cone
   (D) A ball

7. When the moon comes in between the sun and the earth in a straight line, then a solar eclipse is formed. The eclipse occurs because of the __________.
   (A) Formation of a shadow of the earth on the moon
   (B) Formation of a shadow of the moon on the earth
   (C) Reflection of light by the earth
   (D) Reflection of light by the moon

8. In a completely dark room, if you hold up a mirror in front of you, you will see:
(A) Your shadow
(B) A sharp shadow
(C) Your image
(D) No image

9. Sanchit performed the following experiment:

In a dark room, Sanchit took a flashlight, placed a cardboard in front of the flashlight and made a small hole at the centre of the cardboard. Then he switched on the flashlight.

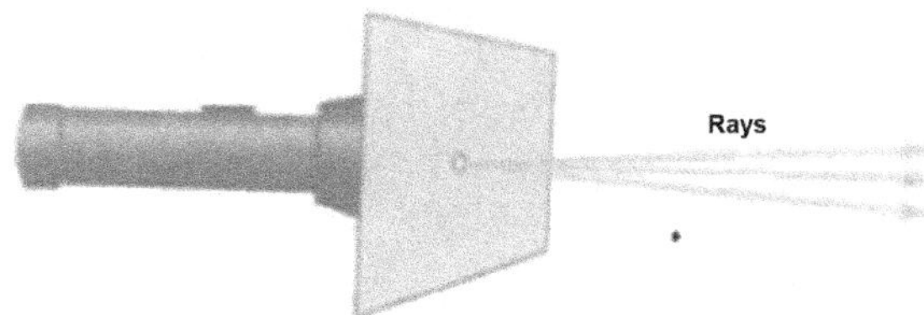

He observed that the light appears to come out from the small hole in a straight line.

Conclusion of the above experiment could be:
(A) Light travels in a straight line
(B) This demonstrates the rectilinear propagation of light
(C) Both (A) and (B)
(D) None of these

10. Butter paper is an example of __________ object.
(A) A transparent   (B) A translucent
(C) An opaque   (D) A luminous

11. Deepti is a dentist. She uses a mirror to focus light on the tooth of a patient. Look at the following pictures and find out that what kind of mirror she uses?

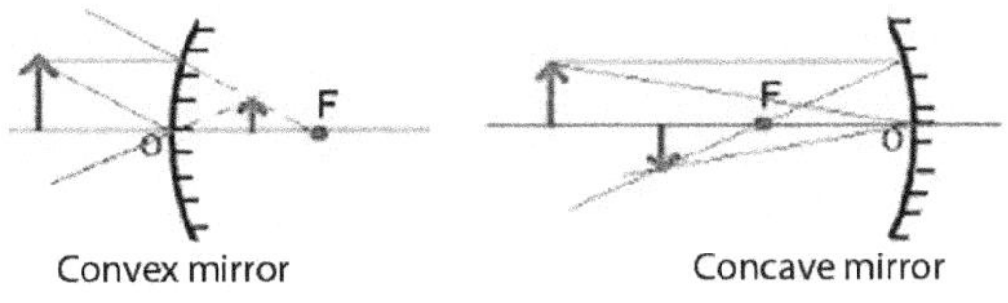

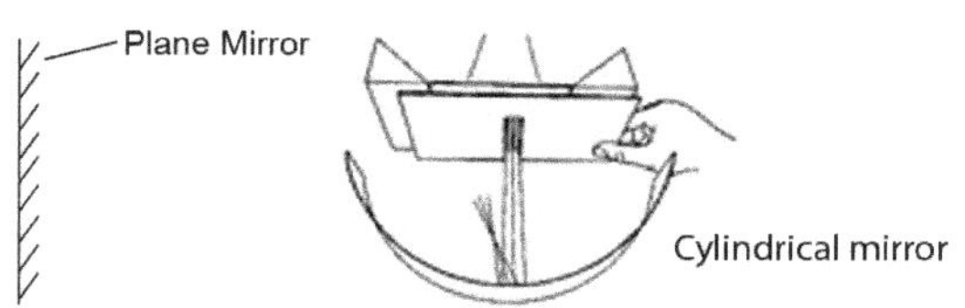

(A) Concave mirror
(B) Convex mirror
(C) Plane mirror
(D) Cylindrical mirror

12. If you stand before a plane mirror, your left hand appears right. This phenomenon is:
(A) The reflection of light
(B) The lateral inversion of light
(C) The shadow formation
(D) The diffusion of light

13. Shadow is formed due to:
(A) The rectilinear propagation of light
(B) The parallel propagation of light
(C) The passing of light through object
(D) All of these

14. Sanchit, Ananya, Ruhi and Rohit are discussing light, shadow and reflection. Choose the incorrect statement.
(A) Sanchit: Light is a form of energy which cannot be seen
(B) Ananya: The image formed by a pin-hole camera is inverted
(C) Ruhi: We see the moon because it is a luminous body
(D) Rohit: Plane mirror is used in periscope

15. Three identical towels of green, blue and red colours are hung on a clothesline in the sun. What would be the colour of shadows of these towels?
(A) The colour of shadow does not depend on the colour of the object. The shadow is always black in colour. So, all three towels will form same colour shadow.
(B) The colour of shadow depends on the colour of the object. So, all three towels will form same colour shadow as their original colours.
(C) The colour of shadow does not depend on the colour of the object, it depends on the thickness of the

object. The shadow is always black in colour. So, all three towels will form same colour shadow.

(D) Both (A) and (C) are correct

16.  

Ambulance seen in a mirror

Look at the two pictures above and choose the correct statement given below.

(A) An image is a reflection of an object in the mirror. Mirrors generally change the direction of light which falls (incident) on them.

(B) When an image of an object is formed in a plane mirror, some reversal of position takes place.

(C) The reversal experienced by an image formed in a plane (flat) mirror is sideways.

(D) All of them

17. 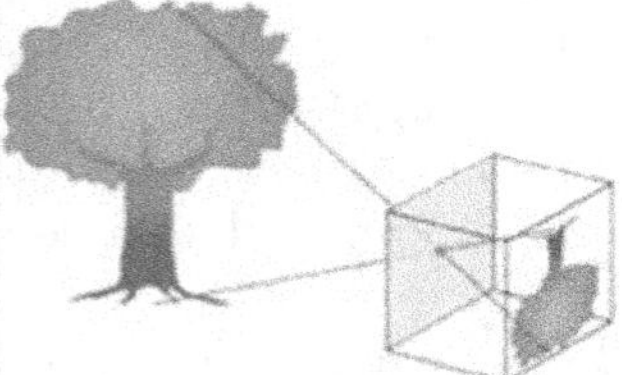

The image given above depicts:

(A) A pinhole camera
(B) A periscope
(C) An eclipse
(D) Both (A) and (C)

18. The following picture is an example of a:

(A) Concave mirror
(B) Convex mirror
(C) Plane mirror
(D) Cylindrical mirror

19. There are two imaginary objects A and B. Object A reflects more than object B. Therefore, object A is likely to be __________ object B.

(A) Made of the same material as
(B) Smoother than
(C) Just as smooth as
(D) Rougher than

20. One night, Ahana was sleeping on her terrace. She looked up at the night sky and observed the things she could see. She made a list of the sources of light in night sky. What should she have written down on her list?

(A) Moon
(B) Clouds
(C) Moon, stars and clouds
(D) Clouds and moon

21. A girl is 2 m away from a plane mirror. If she moves away from the mirror by 0.5 m, what will be the new distance between the object and its image?

(A) 2 m
(B) 1.5 m
(C) 3 m
(D) 2.5 m

22. The focus of a concave mirror is __________.

(A) Real
(B) Virtual
(C) Undefined
(D) At the pole

23. When light falls on the following objects, which among them would show the darkest shadow?

(A) A sheet of thin tissue paper
(B) A glass window
(C) A wooden chopping board
(D) Water in a glass

24. A boy did the following experiment.

He kept a wooden cube in front of a screen. He had three torches with him.

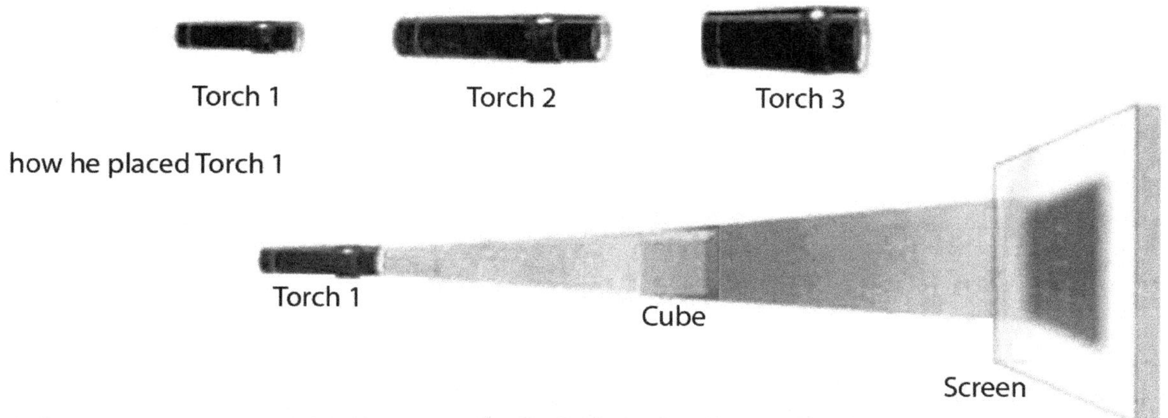

Without changing the position of the cube and the screen, he placed the other two torches one after the other, in the position of torch 1, and saw the shadow.

Which torch will make the largest shadow (umbra) on the screen?

(A) Torch 1

(B) Torch 2

(C) Torch 3

(D) The size of the shadow will be the same for all the three torches.

25. Natural light sources include sun, glowing rocks (lava from volcanoes), and _________.

(A) Fire   (B) Flame

(C) Torch   (D) Fire and flame

26. Are candles, light bulbs, flame, CFL's, tube-lights, kerosene lamps etc. man-made or natural sources of light?

(A) Man-made sources of light

(B) Natural light sources

(C) Some are natural; some are man-made sources of light

(D) None of them

27. Let us take these three objects (glass tumbler, coloured glass and wooden block). Keep them on the table. Now place a pencil box on the other side of these objects.

It was observed that in case of the glass tumbler, the pencil box on the other side can be seen clearly. In case of the coloured glass, the pencil box on the other side cannot be seen very clearly. In the third case, the pencil box is not seen at all from the other side of the wooden block.

So the conclusion can be:

(A) The first object is transparent, the second object is opaque, and the third one is translucent

(B) The first object is transparent, the second object is translucent, and the third one is opaque

(C) The first object is opaque, the second object is translucent, and the third one is transparent

(D) The first object is translucent, the second object is transparent, and the third one is opaque

28. When an object is placed at the focus of a concave mirror, the image will be formed at ____________.
   (A) Infinity
   (B) The focus
   (C) The centre of curvature
   (D) The pole

29. In a lunar eclipse shadow of ________ falls on ________.
   (A) Sun, earth
   (B) Earth, moon
   (C) Moon, sun
   (D) Sun, moon

30. Place a lamp close to a mug and observe its shadow on a table. Notice that the shadow formed has two parts. The darker part of the shadow, is the ________ and the lighter part is the ________.
   (A) Umbra, penumbra
   (B) Penumbra, umbra
   (C) Thicker, thinner
   (D) Only Penumbra

HOTS (ACHIEVERS SECTION)

31. When a lit torchlight is shone on an object X, a shadow is formed on the screen.

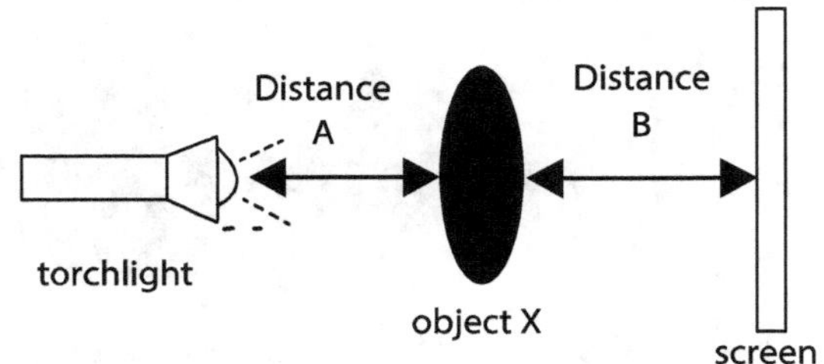

Which of the following options shows how the size of the shadow changes when the distance A and/or distance B changes?

	Size of shadow	Distance A	Distance B
(A)	Bigger	Decreases	Increases
(B)	Smaller	Stays the same	Increases
(C)	Stays the same	Increases	Decreases
(D)	Smaller	Decreases	Stays the same

32. Match column I with column II and choose the correct option:

Column I		Column II
a.	Luminous body	i. Moon
b.	A transparent object	ii. Brick
c.	A translucent object	iii. Star
d.	An opaque object	iv. Clear water
e.	A non-luminous body	v. Thick window glass pan

   (A) a-v, b-iv, c-iii, d-ii, e-i
   (B) a-iii, b-ii, c-v, d-iv, e-i
   (C) a-i, b-iv, c-v, d-ii, e-iii
   (D) a-iii, b-iv, c-v, d-ii, e-i

33. You cannot see the flame of a burning candle by looking through a bent pipe. This is because

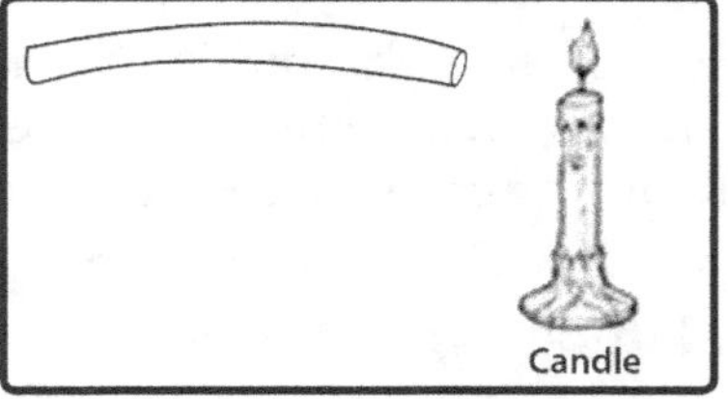

   (A) light gets bent along the pipe.
   (B) light travels in a straight line.
   (C) light gets reflected.
   (D) light gets absorbed.

OLYMPIAD WORKBOOK (NSO) CLASS— 6

34. Observe the diagram given below.

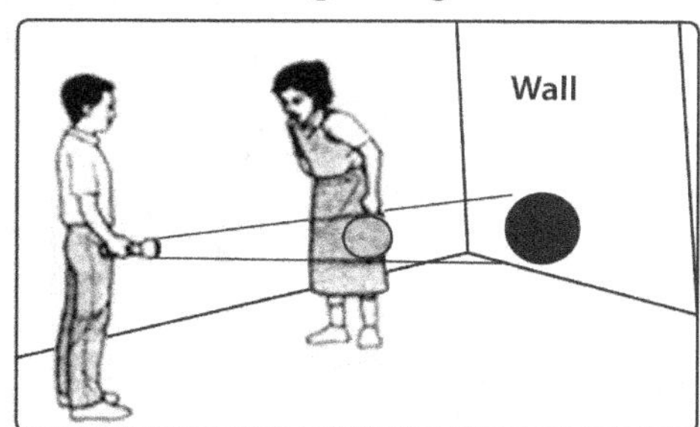

What is proved from the above arrangement?

(A) Light can be refracted.

(B) Light can be reflected.

(C) Light can be blocked.

(D) Light travels faster than sound.

35. Which of the following statements is NOT true regarding shadows?

(A) A shadow gives only the outline of that object.

(B) Shadows are formed due to the blocking of light by an opaque object.

(C) Images are similar to shadows.

(D) A shadow formed is always on the opposite side of the light source.

1.	Ⓐ Ⓑ Ⓒ Ⓓ	8.	Ⓐ Ⓑ Ⓒ Ⓓ	15.	Ⓐ Ⓑ Ⓒ Ⓓ	22	Ⓐ Ⓑ Ⓒ Ⓓ	29.	Ⓐ Ⓑ Ⓒ Ⓓ
2.	Ⓐ Ⓑ Ⓒ Ⓓ	9.	Ⓐ Ⓑ Ⓒ Ⓓ	16.	Ⓐ Ⓑ Ⓒ Ⓓ	23.	Ⓐ Ⓑ Ⓒ Ⓓ	30.	Ⓐ Ⓑ Ⓒ Ⓓ
3.	Ⓐ Ⓑ Ⓒ Ⓓ	10.	Ⓐ Ⓑ Ⓒ Ⓓ	17.	Ⓐ Ⓑ Ⓒ Ⓓ	24.	Ⓐ Ⓑ Ⓒ Ⓓ	31.	Ⓐ Ⓑ Ⓒ Ⓓ
4.	Ⓐ Ⓑ Ⓒ Ⓓ	11.	Ⓐ Ⓑ Ⓒ Ⓓ	18.	Ⓐ Ⓑ Ⓒ Ⓓ	25.	Ⓐ Ⓑ Ⓒ Ⓓ	32.	Ⓐ Ⓑ Ⓒ Ⓓ
5.	Ⓐ Ⓑ Ⓒ Ⓓ	12.	Ⓐ Ⓑ Ⓒ Ⓓ	19.	Ⓐ Ⓑ Ⓒ Ⓓ	26.	Ⓐ Ⓑ Ⓒ Ⓓ	33.	Ⓐ Ⓑ Ⓒ Ⓓ
6.	Ⓐ Ⓑ Ⓒ Ⓓ	13.	Ⓐ Ⓑ Ⓒ Ⓓ	20.	Ⓐ Ⓑ Ⓒ Ⓓ	27.	Ⓐ Ⓑ Ⓒ Ⓓ	34.	Ⓐ Ⓑ Ⓒ Ⓓ
7.	Ⓐ Ⓑ Ⓒ Ⓓ	14.	Ⓐ Ⓑ Ⓒ Ⓓ	21.	Ⓐ Ⓑ Ⓒ Ⓓ	28.	Ⓐ Ⓑ Ⓒ Ⓓ	35.	Ⓐ Ⓑ Ⓒ Ⓓ

ELECTRICITY AND CIRCUITS

LEARNING OBJECTIVES

- ➤ The uses of electricity
- ➤ Concept behind an electric cell
- ➤ The significance of electric circuits
- ➤ Conductors and insulators

MULTIPLE CHOICE QUESTIONS

1. Moving an electron within an electric field would change the _________ the electron.
   (A) Weight of
   (B) Potential energy of
   (C) Amount of charge on
   (D) Mass of

2. Which one of the following statements is false?
   (A) Electricity can pass through copper, steel, iron, nichrome, brass, carbon and aluminium
   (B) Insulators are non-conductors of electricity and they prevent us from getting electrocuted
   (C) Silk, wool, leather and wood are materials that were once alive
   (D) None of the above

3. The diagram below shows an open circuit.

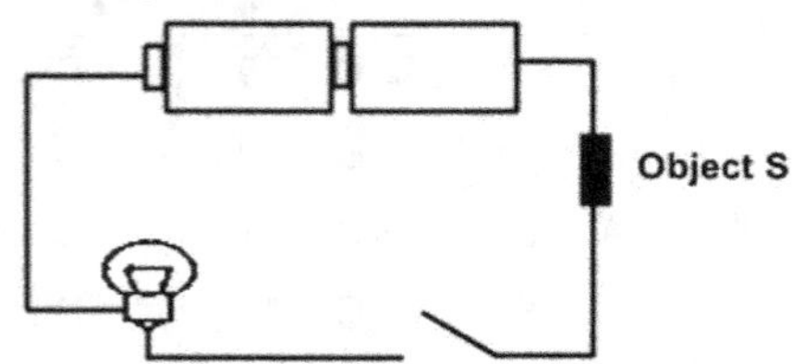

   When the circuit is closed, the light bulb does not light up at all.
   What could be the possible reasons?

1. The light bulb has fused.
2. Object S is a plastic ruler.
3. The batteries are too strong.
4. Object S is an insulator of electricity.
5. The arrangement of batteries is incorrect.
   (A) 1, 2 and 4   (B) 2, 3 and 4
   (C) 1, 2, 4 and 5   (D) 1, 2, 3 and 5

4. Which of the following is the odd one in the group?
   (A) Silver
   (B) Aluminium
   (C) Salt solution
   (D) Ceramic articles

5. The filament of a bulb is usually a:
   (A) Thick straight wire
   (B) Thin straight wire
   (C) Thin wire with many coils
   (D) Thick wire with many coils

6. The main function of a switch is to:
   (A) Make the bulb glow easily
   (B) Allow charges to flow
   (C) Complete or break a circuit
   (D) Prevent electric shocks

OLYMPIAD WORKBOOK (NSO) CLASS— 6

7. Look at the following circuit and read the following paragraph carefully.

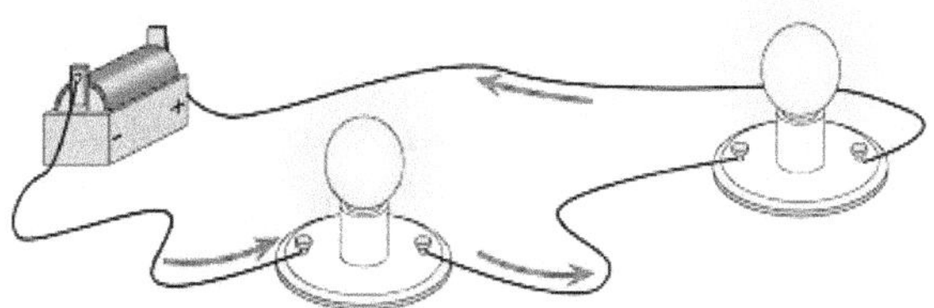

All parts are connected one after another. Electrons flow from the negative terminal of the battery through the loop to the positive terminal.

Which of the following statement is related to the circuit described in the paragraph above?

(A) In a series circuit electricity has only one path to follow

(B) If a light bulb is missing or broken in a series circuit, the other bulb will light

(C) In a parallel circuit, electricity has only one path to follow

(D) Both (A) and (B)

8. If a light bulb is missing or broken in a parallel circuit, will the other bulb light? Explain.

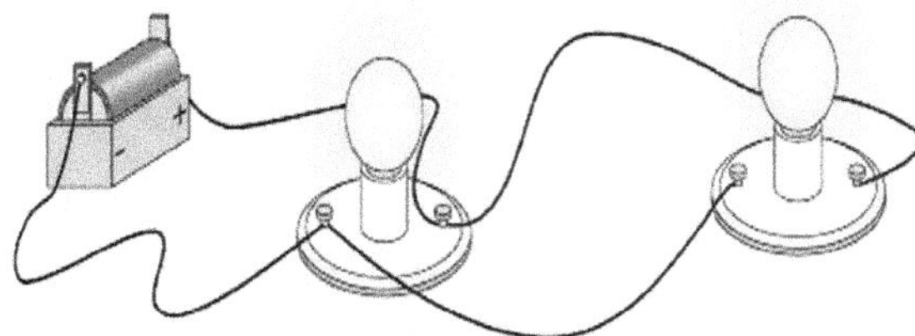

(A) Yes, because the electricity can travel along a different path and avoid the broken bulb.

(B) No, because the path the electricity needs to follow is broken.

(C) Yes, because the path the electricity needs to follow is not broken.

(D) No, because the electricity cannot travel along a different path and avoid the broken bulb.

9. Voltage _________ an electrical circuit.

(A) Goes through

(B) Is expressed across

(C) Is constant throughout

(D) Is the rate at which charges move through

10. If a battery provides a high voltage, it can _________.

(A) Do a lot of work on each charge it encounters

(B) Last a long time

(C) Push a lot of charge through a circuit

(D) Do a lot of work over the course of its lifetime

(For question 11 and 12) Alisha has a mobile phone. Energy is stored in the battery of the phone. The diagram below shows the battery being charged.

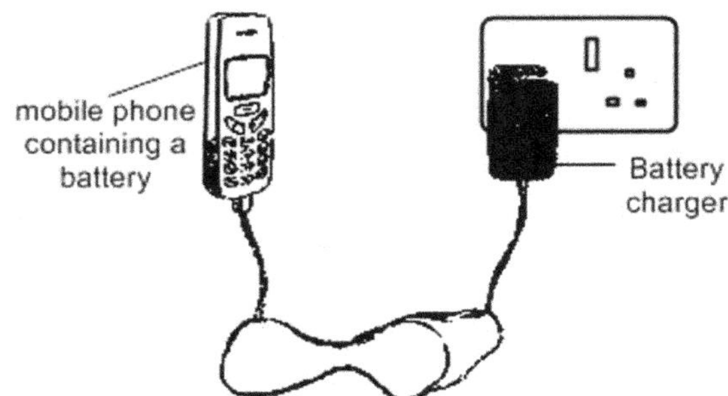

11. The main energy conversion in the battery as it is being charged?

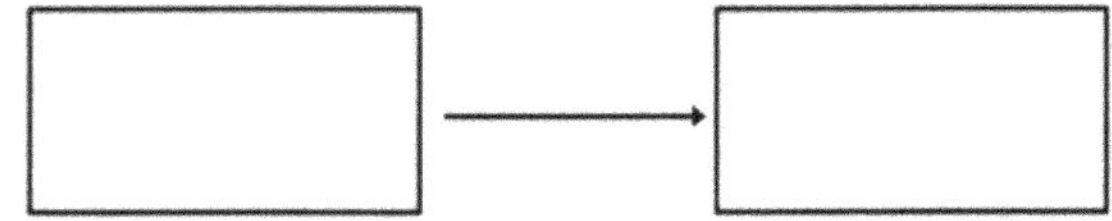

(A) Chemical potential energy ⟶ Electrical energy

(B) Electrical energy ⟶ Potential energy

(C) Electrical energy ⟶ Chemical energy

(D) Potential energy ⟶ Electrical energy

12. When the phone is fully charged, Alisha unplugs the battery charger from the phone. State the energy conversion when the mobile phone rings.

(A) Chemical energy $\longrightarrow$ Electrical energy $\longrightarrow$ Sound energy (+Kinetic energy + Heat energy + Sound energy)

(B) Electrical energy $\longrightarrow$ Chemical potential energy $\longrightarrow$ Sound energy (+Kinetic energy + Heat energy)

(C) Sound energy $\longrightarrow$ Electrical energy $\longrightarrow$ Chemical energy

(D) Sound energy (+Kinetic energy + Heat energy + Sound energy) $\longrightarrow$ Electrical energy $\longrightarrow$ Chemical energy

Use the following diagram for questions no. 13 and 14.

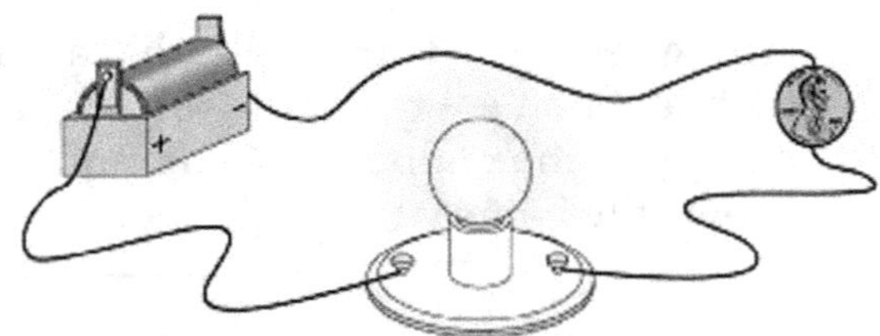

13. What supplies energy in an electric circuit?
   (A) Battery   (B) A conductor
   (C) Light bulb   (D) A wire

14. Which material is a conductor?
   (A) Glass   (B) Silver
   (C) Plastic   (D) Wood

15. Which of these could be used as a resistor in a circuit?
   (A) A rubber eraser
   (B) A pencil
   (C) An electric motor
   (D) A gas engine

16. Which statement is not correct about current electricity?
   (A) The type of electricity that is used to power things we use is called current electricity
   (B) Current electricity is electricity that flows through wires
   (C) Current electricity can flow in any circuit.
   (D) The path that electricity follows is called a circuit

17. In domestic wiring, the neutral wire has which of the following colors?
   (A) Red   (B) Black
   (C) Green   (D) White

18. In a circuit having one bulb, another bulb is added. The new bulb will:
   (A) Get fused
   (B) Not glow
   (C) Glow more brightly
   (D) Glow but less brightly

Direction (19 – 20): Study the circuit diagram below. The bulbs are labelled A, B, C and D. The switches are labeled 1, 2, 3 and 4. Use the diagram to solve questions 19 and 20.

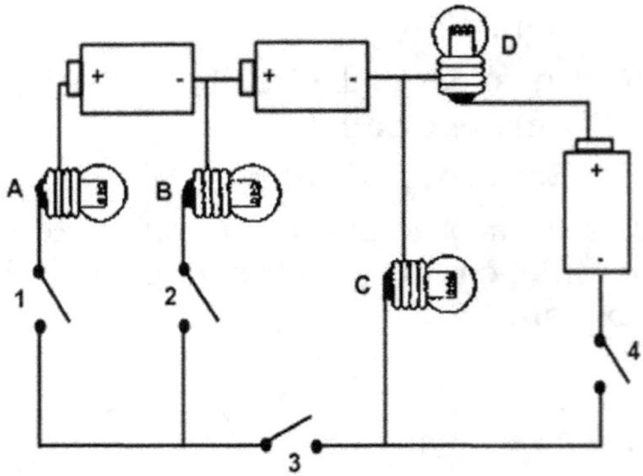

19. Which two switches should be closed so that only bulbs B and C would light up?
   (A) Switches 1 and 2
   (B) Switches 2 and 3
   (C) Switches 3 and 4
   (D) Switches 1 and 3

20. Which bulb(s) will remain lit if bulb D fuses and all the switches are closed?
   (A) Bulbs A, B and C
   (B) Bulbs A and B
   (C) Bulbs A and C
   (D) Bulb D

21. To determine whether an object is a conductor or an insulator, you can build a simple circuit with a battery, bulb, and three pieces of wire.

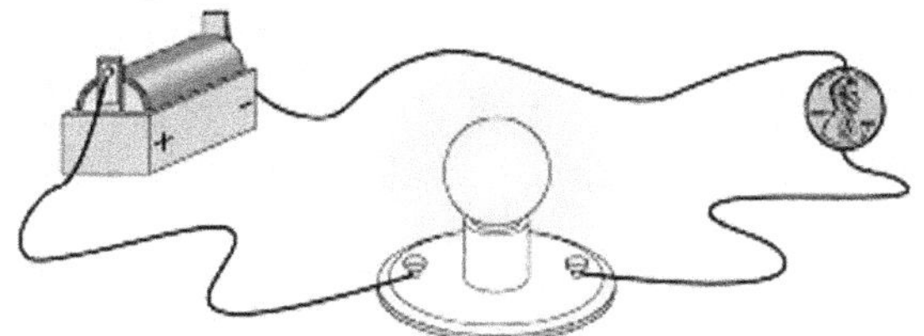

Touch the free ends of the wire to the object you are testing. If the bulb glows up, the object is a ________. If it does not, then the object is an ________.
(A) Rubber, silver
(B) Silver, rubber
(C) Insulator, conductor
(D) Conductor, insulator

22. Which part of the bulb is an insulator?

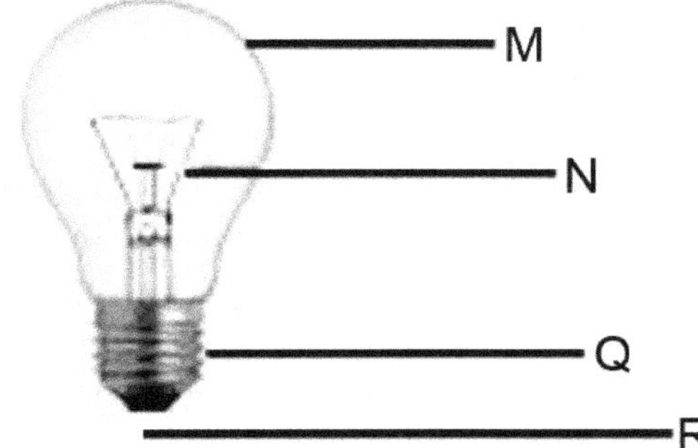

(A) M   (B) N
(C) R   (D) Q

23. The instrument that can measure current is called a/an:
(A) Tester   (B) Ammeter
(C) Resistor   (D) Voltameter

24. The path of electricity is called:
(A) orbit   (B) filament
(C) current   (D) circuit

25. Sanchit's mother warned him to avoid contact with electrical appliances or even electrical outlets when his hands are wet. This is because wet hands can alter ________.

(A) The voltage of the circuit to be higher
(B) The voltage of the circuit to be lower
(C) Your resistance to be higher
(D) Your resistance to be lower

26. Identify the A and B from the following diagram:

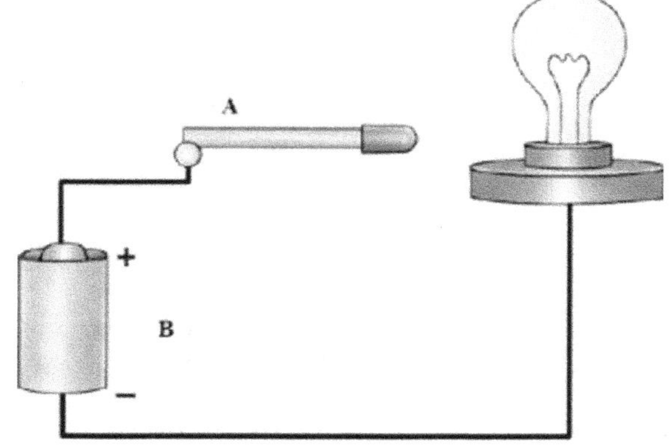

(A) A = Circuit, B = Switch
(B) A = Battery, B = Switch
(C) A = Switch, B = Circuit
(D) A = Switch, B = Battery

27. This wire is the filament of the bulb which becomes red hot and glows when the current is switched on. It is made of a metal called ____________.
(A) Tungsten
(B) Needle
(C) Insulator
(D) Conductor

28. Combination of two or more cells is called a ________.
(A) Circuit
(B) Battery
(C) Switch
(D) None of these

29. The following diagram shows identical lamps X and Y connected in series with a battery. The lamps light with normal brightness. A third lamp Z is connected in parallel lamp X.

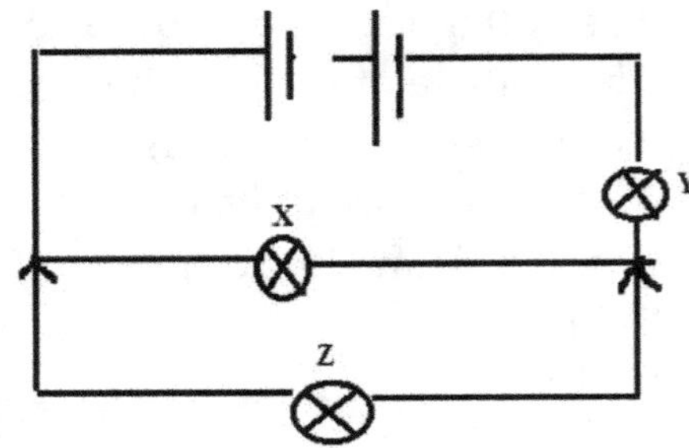

What happens to the brightness of lamp Y?
(A) Very dim
(B) Normal
(C) Brighter than normal
(D) Dimmer than normal

30. If we touch a naked current-carrying wire, we get a shock. This is because our body is a:
(A) Source of electricity
(B) Conductor of electricity
(C) Insulator of electricity
(D) Both (A) and (B)

HOTS (ACHIEVERS SECTION)

31. John prepares an electric circuit. Study the circuit and find out the correct option.

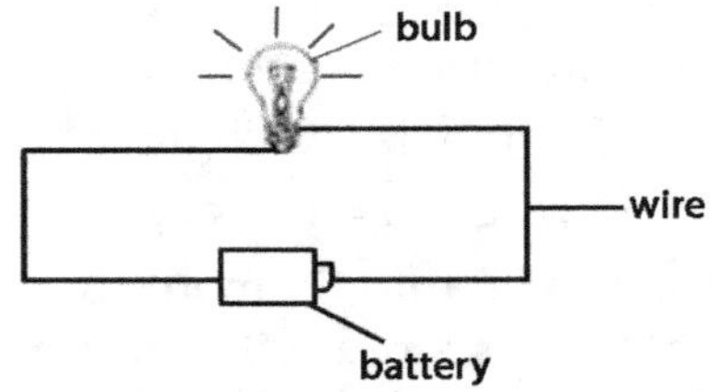

In the circuit given above, electricity passes through the ___________
(A) Wire only
(B) Battery and bulb only
(C) Wire, battery and bulb
(D) Wire and bulb only

32. The following picture shows two circuits with batteries and light bulbs.

Choose the option which explains the above figure correctly.
(A) They are the parallel circuits with electricity flowing along one pathway
(B) They are the series circuits with electricity flowing along one pathway
(C) They are the parallel circuits with electricity flowing along more than one pathway
(D) They are the series circuits with electricity flowing along more than one pathway

33. Identify the circuit diagram in which the bulb does NOT light up.

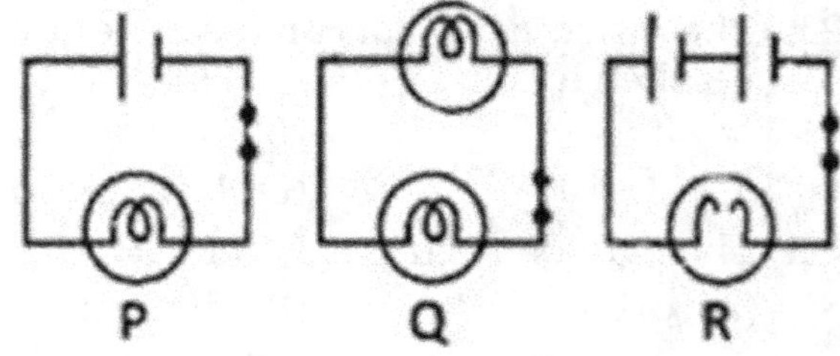

(A) Only P and Q
(B) Only Q and R
(C) Only R and P
(D) P, Q and R

34. Which one of the following is the correct grouping of different materials according to their electrical conductivity?
   - (A) Electrical Insulators - Plastic/wood; Electrical Conductors - Mercury, tungsten
   - (B) Electrical Insulators - Carbon, steel; Electrical Conductors - Iron, paper
   - (C) Electrical Insulators - Copper, gold; Electrical Conductors - Nickel, clay
   - (D) Electrical Insulators - Iron, rubber; Electrical Conductors - Silver, plastic

35. Look at the circuit given below.

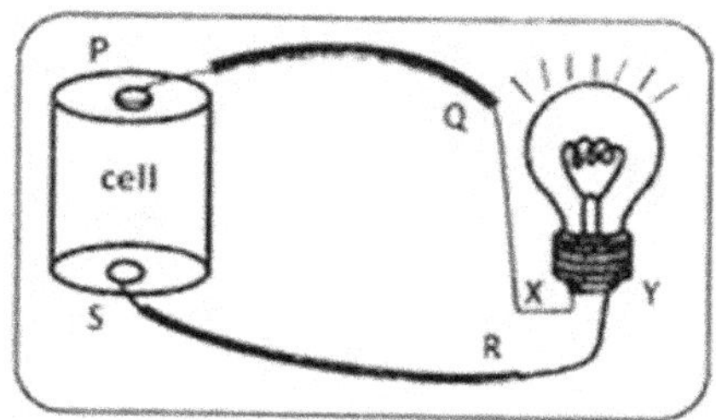

It consists of a cell, a bulb with two terminals X, Y and wires. P, Q, R and S are positions marked. What is the direction of the flow of current?
   - (A) PQRS
   - (B) PSRQ
   - (C) PRQS
   - (D) SQRP

1.	Ⓐ Ⓑ Ⓒ Ⓓ	8.	Ⓐ Ⓑ Ⓒ Ⓓ	15.	Ⓐ Ⓑ Ⓒ Ⓓ	22	Ⓐ Ⓑ Ⓒ Ⓓ	29.	Ⓐ Ⓑ Ⓒ Ⓓ
2.	Ⓐ Ⓑ Ⓒ Ⓓ	9.	Ⓐ Ⓑ Ⓒ Ⓓ	16.	Ⓐ Ⓑ Ⓒ Ⓓ	23.	Ⓐ Ⓑ Ⓒ Ⓓ	30.	Ⓐ Ⓑ Ⓒ Ⓓ
3.	Ⓐ Ⓑ Ⓒ Ⓓ	10.	Ⓐ Ⓑ Ⓒ Ⓓ	17.	Ⓐ Ⓑ Ⓒ Ⓓ	24.	Ⓐ Ⓑ Ⓒ Ⓓ	31.	Ⓐ Ⓑ Ⓒ Ⓓ
4.	Ⓐ Ⓑ Ⓒ Ⓓ	11.	Ⓐ Ⓑ Ⓒ Ⓓ	18.	Ⓐ Ⓑ Ⓒ Ⓓ	25.	Ⓐ Ⓑ Ⓒ Ⓓ	32.	Ⓐ Ⓑ Ⓒ Ⓓ
5.	Ⓐ Ⓑ Ⓒ Ⓓ	12.	Ⓐ Ⓑ Ⓒ Ⓓ	19.	Ⓐ Ⓑ Ⓒ Ⓓ	26.	Ⓐ Ⓑ Ⓒ Ⓓ	33.	Ⓐ Ⓑ Ⓒ Ⓓ
6.	Ⓐ Ⓑ Ⓒ Ⓓ	13.	Ⓐ Ⓑ Ⓒ Ⓓ	20.	Ⓐ Ⓑ Ⓒ Ⓓ	27.	Ⓐ Ⓑ Ⓒ Ⓓ	34.	Ⓐ Ⓑ Ⓒ Ⓓ
7.	Ⓐ Ⓑ Ⓒ Ⓓ	14.	Ⓐ Ⓑ Ⓒ Ⓓ	21.	Ⓐ Ⓑ Ⓒ Ⓓ	28.	Ⓐ Ⓑ Ⓒ Ⓓ	35.	Ⓐ Ⓑ Ⓒ Ⓓ

LEARNING OBJECTIVES

➤ Difference between magnetic and non-magnetic substances
➤ Natural and artificial magnets
➤ Reason behind attraction and repulsion of magnetic poles

MULTIPLE CHOICE QUESTIONS

1. A magnet was placed on a steel table top. A force was exerted on the magnet to move it horizontally across the table from point A to point B as shown in the diagram below.

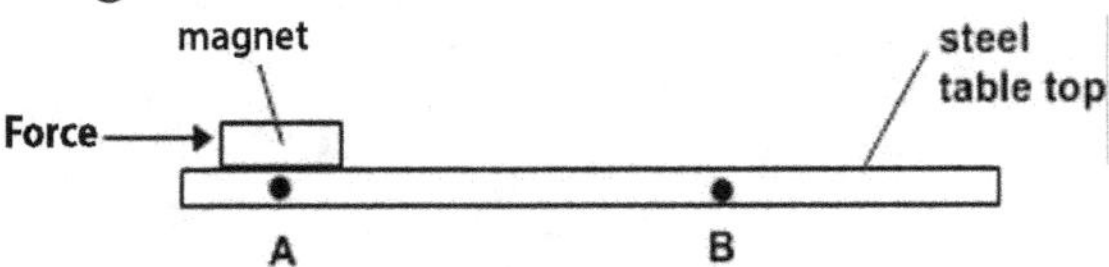

Which of the following force(s) must the push overcome so that the magnet moves from point A to point B?
(A) Frictional force only
(B) Gravitational force only
(C) Frictional force and magnetic force
(D) Frictional force, magnetic force and gravitational force

2. Mini magnetized a metal rod, Y, using a strong magnet. She then put the magnetized rod Y close to a pile of pins and it attracted 12 pins. She wanted to repeat the experiment. However, Mini dropped rod Y three times.

Mini then put rod Y close to the pile of pins again. Which of the following are possible observations she could get?
1. Rod Y could attract less pins.
2. Rod Y could attract more pins.
3. Rod Y could not attract any pins.
4. Rod Y could attract the same number of pins.
(A) 1, 3 and 4
(B) 2 and 4
(C) 1 and 4
(D) 1 and 3

3. Which of the following can be attracted by a magnet?
(A) Wooden piece
(B) Plain pins
(C) Eraser
(D) A piece of cloth

4. Freely suspended magnet always comes to rest in the _____________ direction
(A) North-east
(B) South-west
(C) East-west
(D) North-south

5. The diagram below shows a simple pendulum facing a magnet XY. Attached to the pendulum is another magnet.

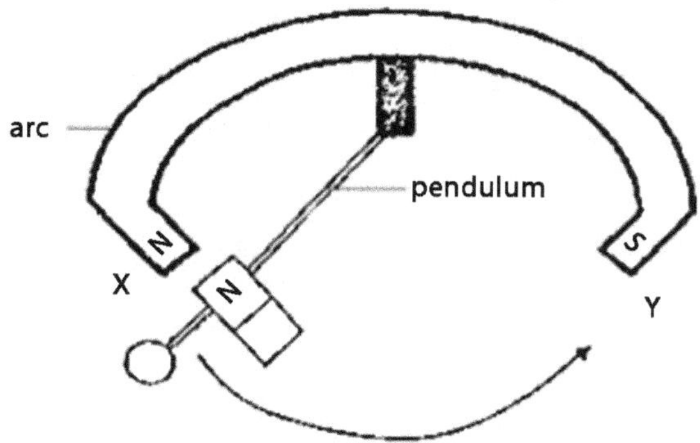

What forces are involved when the pendulum swings from X to Y?
(A) Gravitational force
(B) Magnetic force
(C) Frictional force between the magnet on the pendulum and the arc
(D) Gravitational and magnetic force

6. Which of the following is used to make a permanent magnet?
(A) Nickel
(B) Aluminium
(C) Steel
(D) Iron

7. If the north poles of two magnets are placed near one another, there is a:
(A) Repulsion between them
(B) Attraction between them
(C) No interaction between them
(D) None of these

8. Look at the diagram carefully.

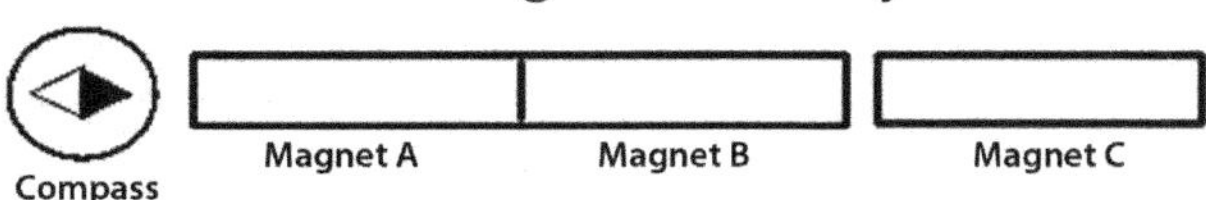

When the three bar magnets are placed near each other, magnet A and B are attracted to each other but magnet B and C repel each other.

Which of the following diagrams shows the correct poles for Magnet A and Magnet C?

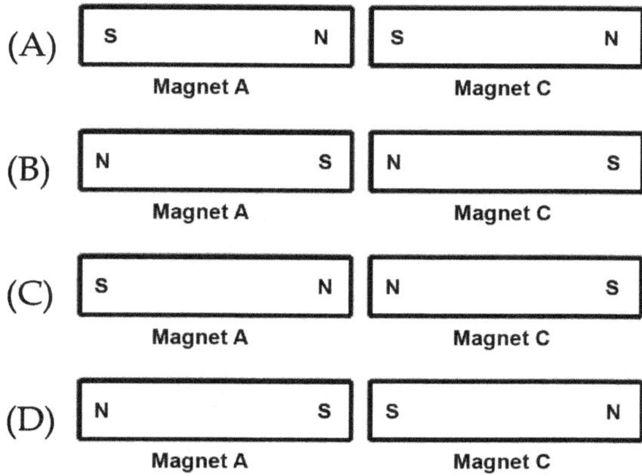

9. A bar magnet is cut into four pieces. Which of the following observations would be true?
(A) Each piece is a complete magnet
(B) Each piece loses magnetism
(C) Some pieces of them have only South Pole
(D) Some pieces of them have only North Pole

10. A bar of steel can be permanently magnetized by:
(A) Rubbing a bar magnet at its ends
(B) Rubbing a bar magnet at its centre
(C) Rubbing a bar magnet with it along the length
(D) None of these

11. An artificial magnet which is used for finding geographical directions is called:
(A) Magnetic compass
(B) Electromagnet
(C) Bar magnet
(D) Horseshoe

12. The accurate test for magnetism is:
(A) Attraction and repulsion
(B) Attraction only
(C) Repulsion only
(D) None of the above

13. Shia had four magnets as shown below.

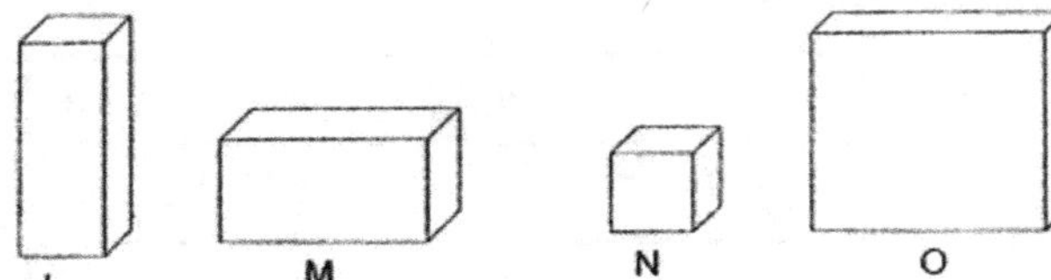

She placed the magnets near a pile of staples and recorded her observation in the table below.

Magnet	Distance between magnets and staples (cm)	Number of staples attracted
L	2	12
M	5	11
N	6	12
O	2	11

Which of the following about magnet is correct?

(A) Magnet L is stronger than magnet M

(B) Magnet N has the strongest magnetic strength

(C) The bigger the magnet, the stronger the magnetism

(D) Magnet M and magnet O have the same magnetic strength

14. Alisha found three objects and wanted to test if they were magnets. She bought a magnet from the school bookshop and placed it next to each of the objects. This is what she observed.

Object	Observation
Object A	No reaction
Object B	Repelled
Object C	Attracted

Which of the following object(s) is definitely a magnet?

(A) Object B

(B) Object C

(C) Objects A and C

(D) Objects B and A

15. A student tries to magnetize a short steel rod. Which of the following tests will show that she has succeeded?

(A) Both ends of a magnet attract the rod

(B) One end of a magnet repels the rod

(C) When freely suspended, the rod points in any direction

(D) The rod picks up a small piece of paper

16. There are the following number of poles in a magnet:

(A) One   (B) Four

(C) Two   (D) Three

17. Loadstone is an example of:

(A) A natural magnet

(B) An artificial magnet

(C) An electromagnet

(D) None of these

18. The attraction of iron filings by the poles of a magnet is:

(A) Minimum   (B) Maximum

(C) Zero   (D) Medium

19. The presence of magnetism in a magnet is due to:

(A) Its basic structural property

(B) Due to the molecular arrangement in a particular order

(C) Due to the molecular arrangement in the form of a closed chain

(D) None of these

20. An effective length of a magnet is:

(A) Either greater or smaller depending on the nature of the material

(B) Equal to its geometric length

(C) Smaller than its geometric length

(D) Equal to its geometric length

21. The classification chart below shows how some things can be classified.

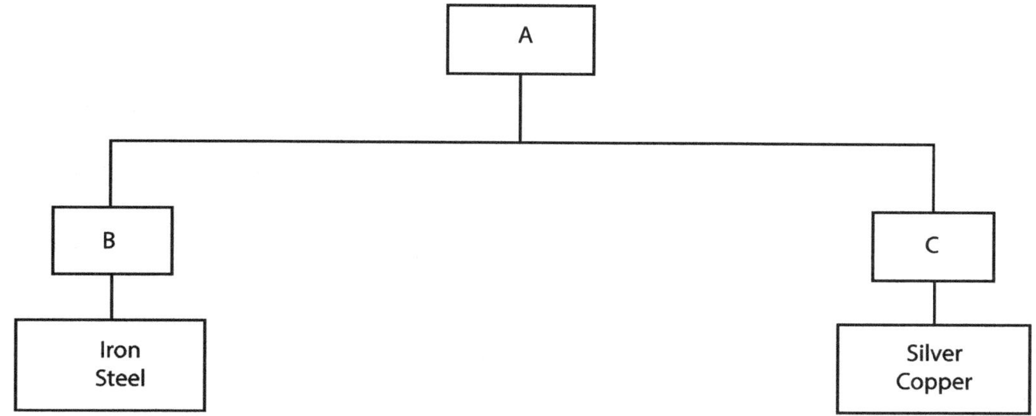

Which one of the following descriptions about A, B and C is correct?

	A	**B**	**C**
(A)	Magnets	Can be repelled by magnet	Cannot be repelled by a magnet
(B)	Metals	Can be made into magnets	Cannot be made into magnets
(C)	Metals	Non-conductor of heat	Conductor of heat
(D)	Materials	Non-conductor of electricity	Conductor of electricity

22. An object P is brought near a bar magnet and its end marked Z is attracted to the South Pole of the magnet as shown below.

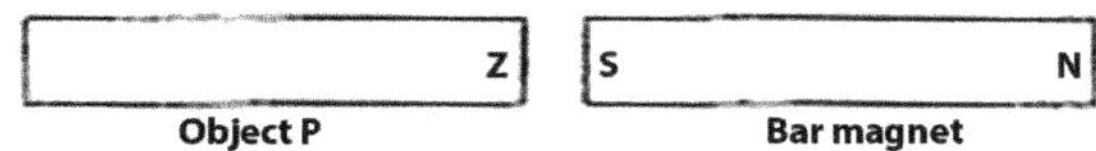

Based on the information given, object P could be a ________________.

(A) Copper rod and magnet
(B) Nickel rod and Copper rod
(C) Magnet and Nickel rod
(D) None of the above

23. Yuvi performed an experiment. He placed a sheet of plastic between two nails and a magnet as shown in the diagram below. The nails were attached to the magnet. Then Michael placed more and more similar sheets of plastic until the nails could no longer be attracted by the magnet.

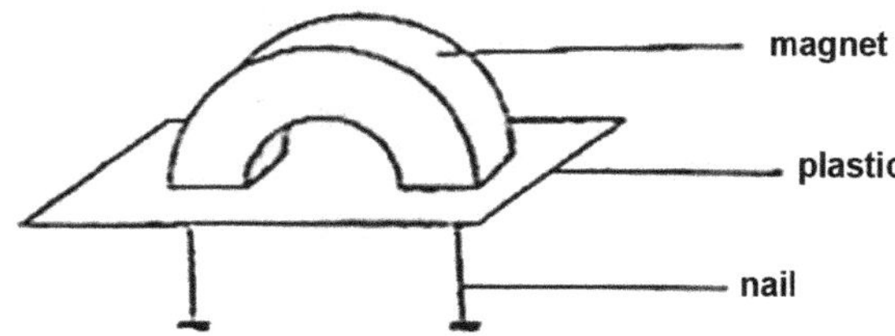

What is the aim of Michael's experiment?
(A) To find out if the plastic is magnetic
(B) To find out if the nails are magnetic
(C) To find out the strength of the magnet
(D) To find out the part of the magnet that has the strongest pull

24. One day Sahil found an iron disc at the bottom of a heavy plastic tank half filled with oil as shown in the diagram below. He successfully removed the iron disc out of the tank with a magnet.

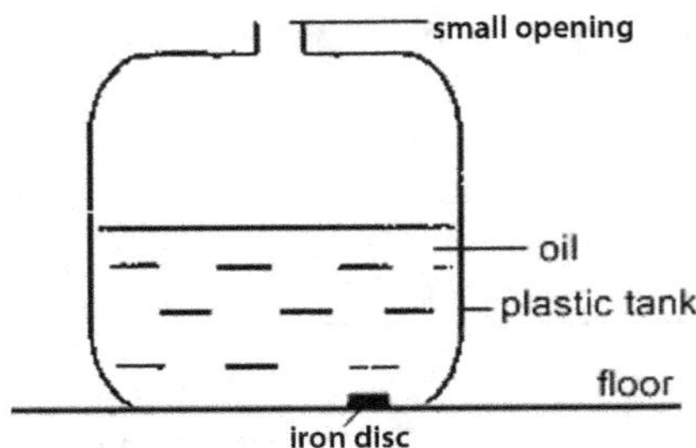

Which one of the following statements is correct?

(A) Oil was magnetised by the magnet

(B) Magnetism can pass through iron disc

(C) Oil and plastic tank were magnetised by the magnet

(D) Magnetism can pass through the oil and plastic tank

25. A magnet can be made weaker by:

(A) Playing with it

(B) Keeping it wrapped in a cotton cloth

(C) Using it as a hammer

(D) Keeping it in a cool room

26. We should not store a floppy disc near a magnet. Why?

(A) Because the magnet will break the disk

(B) Because the magnet will rust

(C) Because the magnet will become weaker

(D) Because the information in the disk may be erased

27. In many houses we can find a magnet instead of a lock or a bolt in the doors. Magnets are used in such places mainly to:

(A) Ensure safety

(B) Make the articles look beautiful

(C) Facilitate frequent usage

(D) Make the articles airtight

28. Which of the following does not contain a magnet in it?

(A) Radio   (B) Fan

(C) Torch   (D) None

29. The best way to separate a mixture of sand and iron fillings is by:

(A) Using compass

(B) Filtration

(C) Sedimentation

(D) Magnetic separation

30. The people who made mariner's compass for the first time were:

(A) Indians   (B) Europeans

(C) Chinese   (D) Egyptians

HOTS (ACHIEVERS SECTION)

31. Shivani wanted to find out whether a nail was magnetized. She put the nail near a magnet, a compass and a paper clip. Then, she recorded the observations as follows:

i. It could move the compass needle.

ii. It attracted the paper clip.

iii. It attracted the magnet.

iv. It repelled the magnet.

From which of the observations can she ensure that the nail was magnetized?

(A) i only   (B) i and ii only

(C) ii and ii only   (D) All of the above

32. Look the following compass carefully

Now, observe the following arrangements of magnet and compass and find out which of the following shows the direction of compass when they are put near a bar magnet?

(A)  magnet 

(B) magnet

(C)  magnet 

(D) magnet 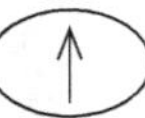

OLYMPIAD WORKBOOK (NSO) CLASS– 6

33. Which part of a bar magnet will attract the maximum number of iron nails when it is brought near a heap of iron nails?
   (A) North pole
   (B) South pole
   (C) Middle portion
   (D) Near both poles

34. Match Column-I with Column-II and select the correct answer using the codes given below the columns.

Column-I	Column-II
(A) North-seeking pole	(p) Pole of a freely suspended magnet which points to south.
(B) South-seeking pole	(q) cannot exists independently.
(C) Electromagnet	(r) Pole of a freely suspended magnet which points to north.
(D) Magnetic poles	(s) are used to lift heavy weights.

   (A) A→(p); B→(q); C→(r); D→(s)
   (B) A→(p); B→(r); C→(q); D→(s)
   (C) A→(s); B→(p); C→(r); D→(q)
   (D) A→(r); B→(p); C→(s); D→(q)

35. Letters A, B, C, and D represent locations on a bar magnet.

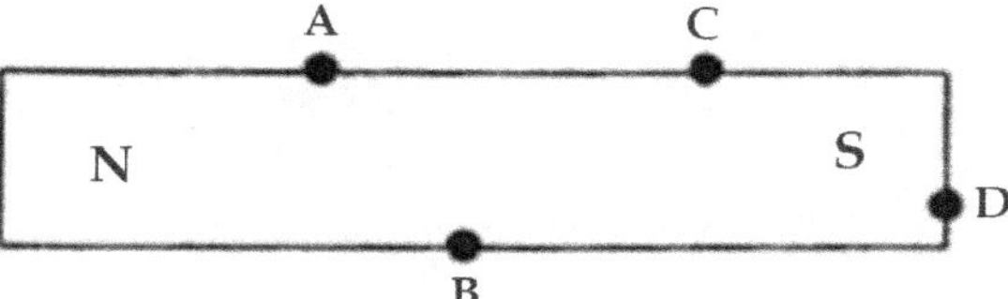

Which location has the greatest magnetic force?
   (A) A
   (B) B
   (C) C
   (D) D

OUR ENVIRONMENT

LEARNING OBJECTIVES

- ➤ Naturals Resources
- ➤ Water

MULTIPLE CHOICE QUESTIONS

1. Which of the following is not paired correctly?
   - (A) Whales-blowholes
   - (B) Deer-Long ears
   - (C) Mountain goat-strong hooves
   - (D) Frogs-oceans

2. The animals that stay deeper in the ocean do not have
   - a. Streamlined shape
   - b. Gills
   - c. Blowholes
   - d. Strong hindlimbs
   - (A) All
   - (B) a, c and d
   - (C) Only b and c
   - (D) a, b and c

3. Adaptation which is not possessed by the deer to survive in the forest is
   - (A) strong teeth
   - (B) eyes in front
   - (C) high speed
   - (D) long ears

4. Which of the following organisms has aerial habitat?
   - (A) Bat
   - (B) Fish
   - (C) Cactus
   - (D) Camel

5. Choose the odd one out.
   - (A) Camel
   - (B) Fish
   - (C) Octopus
   - (D) Sea horse

6. Which of the following is/are abiotic component(s) of ecosystem?
   - (A) Insects
   - (B) Birds
   - (C) Plants
   - (D) Soil

7. Which of the following is a biotic component of ecosystem?
   - (A) Temperature
   - (B) Cactus
   - (C) Rainfall
   - (D) Wind

8. Which of the following organisms is called autotroph?
(A) Earthworm
(B) Grass
(C) Cow
(D) Human

9. Which of the following organisms is a herbivore?
(A) Rabbit
(B) Lion
(C) Eagle
(D) Fox

10. The organisms that prepare their own food are called
(A) heterotrophs
(B) autotrophs
(C) carnivores
(D) herbivores

11. The organisms that feed on both plant and animal products are called _________.
(A) Herbivores
(B) Carnivores
(C) Omnivores
(D) Consumers

12. Which of the following organisms are called decomposers?
(A) Fungi
(B) Tigers
(C) Cats
(D) Dogs

13. Which of the following organisms is present at the top of the trophic level?
(A) Deer
(B) Tiger
(C) Snake
(D) Rat

14. Which of the following is the correct sequence of organisms in a food chain?
(A) Grass → Rat → Eagle → Snake
(B) Grass → Rabbit → Deer → Tiger
(C) Grass → Deer → Elephant → Tiger
(D) Grass → Rat → Snake → Eagle

15. Which of the following organisms are called producers?
(A) Plants
(B) Insects
(C) Birds
(D) Animals

16. Which of the following organisms are called omnivorous?
(A) Cockroach
(B) Rabbit
(C) Deer
(D) Fox

17. Which of the following organisms are called chemo-autotrophs?
(A) Plants
(B) Nitrobacteria
(C) Cows
(D) Humans

18. Humans are
(A) herbivores
(B) carnivores
(C) omnivores
(D) autotrophic

19. Which of the following comprises an artificial habitat to conserve wildlife?
(A) Sanctuaries
(B) Zoo
(C) National Park
(D) Biosphere Reserves

20. Which of the following is the best example of a mini ecosystem?
(A) Water bottle
(B) Kitchen
(C) Pond
(D) Aquarium

21. A, B and C are three plants. Leaves are modified into spines in A, B has needle like leaves and C has hollow stems. Which of the following sentences can you conclude about A, B or C?

    (A) In C, leaves are modified into spines.

    (B) B has small roots.

    (C) A grows in an area where there is very less rainfall.

    (D) C is cone shaped.

22. An aquatic bird would most probably show which of the following adaptation?

    a. Webbed feet

    b. Strong back legs

    c. Hollow bones

    d. Furry coat

    (A) a, b and c

    (B) c and d

    (C) a and b

    (D) a and c

23. Sourabh bought an aquatic plant from a nearby pond. On seeing the plant, his mother concluded that it is a totally submerged plant. How did she reach at that conclusion?

    (A) By seeing the stem of the plant.

    (B) By seeing the leaf of the plant.

    (C) By seeing root of the plant.

    (D) By seeing both root and stem of the plant.

24. In a fancy dress competition three students came with the following posters:

    Student 1: Chicken becomes hen

    Student 2: Abdomen moves while resting

    Student 3: Get rid of wastes

    What do these 3 sentences signify respectively?

    (A) Growth, Respiration, Excretion

    (B) Reproduction, Breathing, Excretion

    (C) Growth, Breathing, Excretion

    (D) Reproduction, Respiration, Excretion

25. A and B are two processes carried out by plants. Process A produces more oxygen compared to its utilisation by the process of B and occurs during day. The process of B continues day and night. What does A and B represent respectively?

    (A) Respiration, photosynthesis

    (B) Transpiration, photosynthesis, day

    (C) Photosynthesis, respiration

    (D) Transpiration, respiration

Darken Your Choice with HB Pencil

	A B C D		A B C D		A B C D		A B C D		A B C D
1.	Ⓐ Ⓑ Ⓒ Ⓓ	6.	Ⓐ Ⓑ Ⓒ Ⓓ	11.	Ⓐ Ⓑ Ⓒ Ⓓ	16	Ⓐ Ⓑ Ⓒ Ⓓ	21.	Ⓐ Ⓑ Ⓒ Ⓓ
2.	Ⓐ Ⓑ Ⓒ Ⓓ	7.	Ⓐ Ⓑ Ⓒ Ⓓ	12.	Ⓐ Ⓑ Ⓒ Ⓓ	17.	Ⓐ Ⓑ Ⓒ Ⓓ	22.	Ⓐ Ⓑ Ⓒ Ⓓ
3.	Ⓐ Ⓑ Ⓒ Ⓓ	8.	Ⓐ Ⓑ Ⓒ Ⓓ	13.	Ⓐ Ⓑ Ⓒ Ⓓ	18.	Ⓐ Ⓑ Ⓒ Ⓓ	23.	Ⓐ Ⓑ Ⓒ Ⓓ
4.	Ⓐ Ⓑ Ⓒ Ⓓ	9.	Ⓐ Ⓑ Ⓒ Ⓓ	14.	Ⓐ Ⓑ Ⓒ Ⓓ	19.	Ⓐ Ⓑ Ⓒ Ⓓ	24.	Ⓐ Ⓑ Ⓒ Ⓓ
5.	Ⓐ Ⓑ Ⓒ Ⓓ	10.	Ⓐ Ⓑ Ⓒ Ⓓ	15.	Ⓐ Ⓑ Ⓒ Ⓓ	20.	Ⓐ Ⓑ Ⓒ Ⓓ	25.	Ⓐ Ⓑ Ⓒ Ⓓ

LOGICAL REASONING

LEARNING OBJECTIVES

- Pattern type questions
- Concept of Analogy
- Concept of Series Completion
- Concept of Odd One Out
- Letter Coding
- Number/Symbol Coding
- Alphabetical Order

- Alphabetical Quibble
- Number Test
- Concept of Direction Sense Test
- Concept of Essential Element
- Mirror Image of Letters
- Concept of Embedded Figure
- Concept of Figure Puzzles

MULTIPLE CHOICE QUESTIONS

Study the pattern and find the missing number.

1.

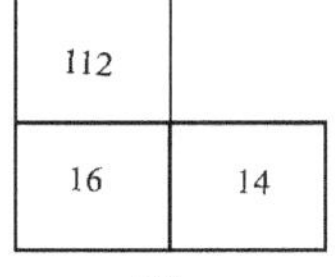

| | | |
| (i) | (ii) | (iii) |

(A) 14   (B) 16
(C) 18   (D) 21

2.

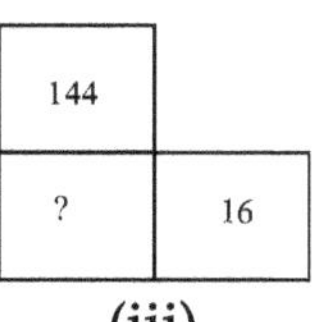

(i)   (ii)   (iii)

(A) 98   (B) 96
(C) 99   (D) 108

3.

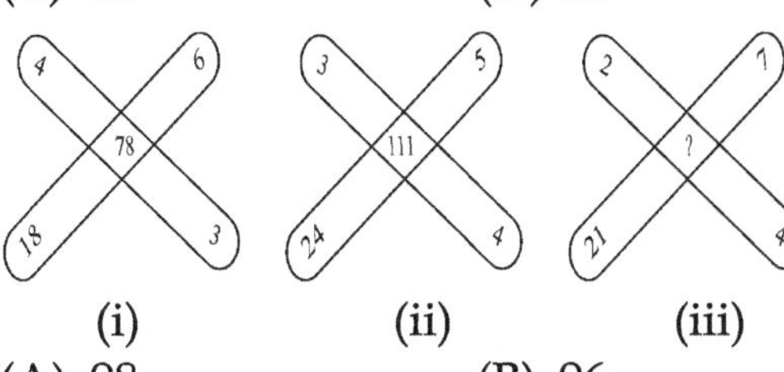

(A) 121   (B) 149
(C) 169   (D) 196

4.

2   3   4   5   6   7

36   400   ?
(i)   (ii)   (iii)

(A) 1594   (B) 1764
(C) 1664   (D) 1784

5.

14 24   23 35   34 45

36   55   ?
(i)   (ii)   (iii)

(A) 75   (B) 76
(C) 77   (D) 78

Directions (6 – 10): In each of the following questions, there is a certain relationship between two given words on one side of : : and one word is given on the other side of : :

Find out the word from the given alternatives, having the same relation with this word as the words of the given pair bear.

6. Physician : Treatment :: Judge : ?
   (A) Punishment   (B) Judgement
   (C) Lawyer   (D) Court

7. Ice : Coldness :: Earth : ?
   (A) Weight   (B) Jungle
   (C) Gravity   (D) Sea

8. Race : Fatigue :: Fast : ?
   (A) Food   (B) Laziness
   (C) Hunger   (D) Race

9. Peace : Chaos :: Creation : ?
   (A) Build   (B) Construction
   (C) Destruction   (D) Manufacture

10. Tiger : Forest :: Otter : ?
    (A) Cage   (B) Sky
    (C) Nest   (D) Water

Direction (11–15): Identify the pattern in the given series and choose the correct option to replace the question mark.

11. 67, 74, 81, 88, 95, ?
    (A) 101   (B) 102
    (C) 103   (D) 104

12. 109, 101, 94, 88, 83, ?
    (A) 78   (B) 79
    (C) 80   (D) 81

13. 9, 25, 49, 81, 121, ?
    (A) 141   (B) 144
    (C) 161   (D) 169

14. 3, 8, 15, 24, 35, 48, ?
    (A) 61   (B) 62
    (C) 63   (D) 64

15. 6, 12, 24, 48, 96, 192, ?
    (A) 384   (B) 386
    (C) 388   (D) 392

Direction: Choose the odd one out from the following.

16. (A) History   (B) Physics
    (C) Civics   (D) Geography

17. (A) Mosque   (B) Temple
    (C) Mantery   (D) Church

18. (A) Operating system (B) Hard disk
    (C) Printer   (D) Pendrive

19. (A) Ruby   (B) Marble
    (C) Sapphire   (D) Diamond

20. (A) Peel   (B) Fry
    (C) Roast   (D) Bake

21. If TRUTH is coded as SUQSTVSUGI, then the code for FALSE will be __________.
    (A) FGZBKNRTDF
    (B) EGZBKMRDE
    (C) EGZKMRTDF
    (D) EGZBKMRTDF

22. In a certain code, INACTIVE is written as VITCANIE. How is COMPUTER written in the same code?
    (A) UTEPMOCR   (B) MOCPETUR
    (C) ETUPMOCR   (D) PMOCRETU

23. In a certain code, COVALENT, is written as BWPDUOFM and FORM is written as PGNS. How will SILVER be written in that code?
    (A) MJTSFW   (B) MJTWFS
    (C) KHRSFW   (D) None of these

24. In a certain code, VISHWANATHAN is written as NAAWTHHSANIV. How is KARUMAKARAMA written in that code?
    (A) KAAMRAURMAAK
    (B) NKKRAMKRAUK
    (C) RURNKAAUNAK
    (D) AKNUARRAANKA

25. In a certain code, MOTHER is written as ONHURF. How will ANSWER be written in that code?
    (A) NBWRRF   (B) MAVSPE
    (C) NBWTRF   (D) NBXSSE

Directions (26 – 30): Arrange the given words in alphabetical order and choose the one that comes first.

26. (A) Guarantee   (B) Group
    (C) Groan   (D) Grotesque

27. (A) Necessary   (B) Nature
    (C) Naval   (D) Nautical
28. (A) Foment   (B) Foetus
    (C) Foliage   (D) Forceps
29. (A) Deuce   (B) Dew
    (C) Devise   (D) Dexterity
30. (A) Quarter   (B) Quarrel
    (C) Quarry   (D) Qualify

31. In the series given below, how many 8's are there each of which is exactly divisible by its immediate preceding as well as succeeding numbers?

    2 8 4 3 8 5 4 8 2 6 7 8 4 6 2 8 4 1 7 ?

    (A) 1   (B) 2
    (C) 3   (D) 4

32. How many 5's are there in the following number sequence which are immediately preceded by 7 and immediately followed by 8?

    7 5 5 8 4 5 7 8 4 5 9 8 7 5 8 7 8 4 3 2 5 8 7 6?

    (A) 1   (B) 2
    (C) 3   (D) None of these

33. In the given series 7 4 5 7 6 8 4 2 1 3 5 1 7 6 8 9 2 how many pairs of alternate numbers have a difference of 2?

    (A) 1   (B) 2
    (C) 3   (D) 4

34. How many 4's are there preceded by 7 but not followed by 5?

    5 9 3 1 7 4 5 8 4 6 7 4 3 1 4 7 4 2 8 7 4 1 ?

    (A) 1   (B) 2
    (C) 3   (D) 4

35. How many 5's are there which are in between two even numbers.

    4 3 5 6 4 5 2 3 4 5 8 5 4 6 7 5 2 6 9 8 5 1 2 4 5

    (A) 1   (B) 2
    (C) 3   (D) 4

36. One morning after sunrise, Mohan was standing facing a pole. The shadow of the pole falls exactly to his right. Which direction was he facing?
    (A) North   (B) South
    (C) East   (D) West

37. If south – east is called east, north – west is called west, south – west is called south and so on what will north be called?
    (A) South   (B) North East
    (C) East   (D) North West

38. A, B, C and D are playing a game of carom. A & C and B & D are partners. D is to the right of C, who is facing west, then in which direction B is facing?
    (A) East   (B) West
    (C) North   (D) South

39. Rajesh is 40 m south – west of Rohit. Rakesh is 40 m south-east of Rohit. Then Rakesh is in which direction of Rajesh?
    (A) East   (B) West
    (C) South   (D) North

40. Pravin wants to go to the college. He starts from his home which is in the east and comes to a crossing. The road to the left ends in a theatre, straight ahead in the hospital. In which direction is the college?
    (A) North   (B) South
    (C) East   (D) West

Directions (41 to 45): Find the word that names a necessary part of the underlined word.

41. <u>Knowledge</u>
    (A) School   (B) Teacher
    (C) Textbook   (D) Learning
42. <u>Culture</u>
    (A) Civility   (B) Education
    (C) Agriculture   (D) Customs
43. <u>Antique</u>
    (A) Rarity   (B) Artefact
    (C) Aged   (D) Prehistoric
44. <u>Dimension</u>
    (A) Compass   (B) Ruler
    (C) Inch   (D) Measure
45. <u>Purchase</u>
    (A) Trade   (B) Money
    (C) Bank   (D) Acquisition

Directions (46 – 50): In each of the following questions, there is combination of alphabet or number followed by four alternatives. Choose the alternative which most clearly resembles the mirror image of the given combination.

46. TERMINATE
    (a) TERMINATE (mirror)   (b) TERMINATE (mirror)
    (c) TERMINATE (mirror)   (d) TERMINATE (mirror)

47. 1965INDOPAK
    (a) 1965INDOPAK (mirror)   (b) 1965INDOPAK (mirror)
    (c) 1965INDOPAK (mirror)   (d) 1965INDOPAK (mirror)

48. NATIONAL
    (a) NATIONAL (mirror)   (b) NATIONAL (mirror)
    (c) NATIONAL (mirror)   (d) NATIONAL (mirror)

49. UTZFY6KH
    (a) HK6YFZTU (mirror)   (b) HK6YFZTU (mirror)
    (c) HK6YFZTU (mirror)   (d) HK6YFZTU (mirror)

50. SUPERVISOR
    (a) SUPERVISOR (mirror)   (b) SUPERVISOR (mirror)
    (c) SUPERVISOR (mirror)   (d) SUPERVISOR (mirror)

Directions (51 - 55): Analyze the set of figures and choose the correct option that contains figure X.

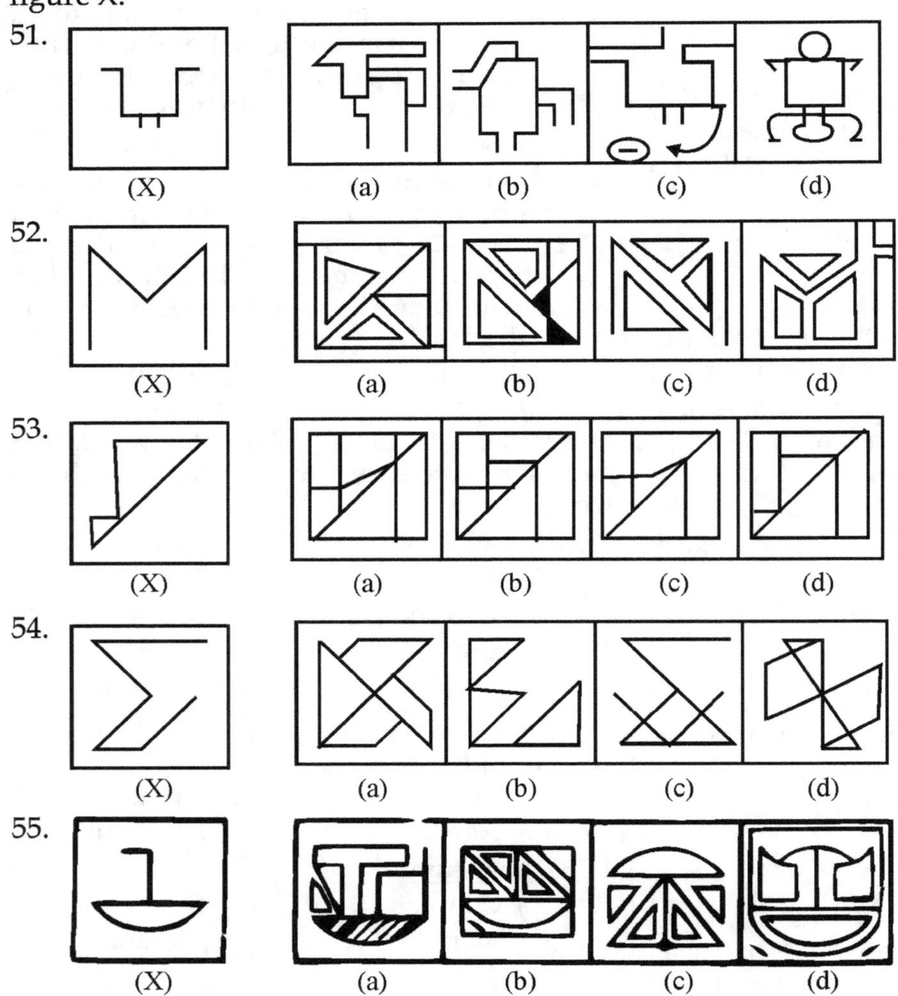

51. (X) (a) (b) (c) (d)

52. (X) (a) (b) (c) (d)

53. (X) (a) (b) (c) (d)

54. (X) (a) (b) (c) (d)

55. (X) (a) (b) (c) (d)

Directions (56 – 60): In this type of questions, a figure or a matrix is given in which some numbers are filled according to a rule. A place is left blank or a question mark put. You have to find out a character (a number or a letter) from the given possible answers which may be filled in the blank space or may replace the question mark.

56. Which option will replace the question mark?

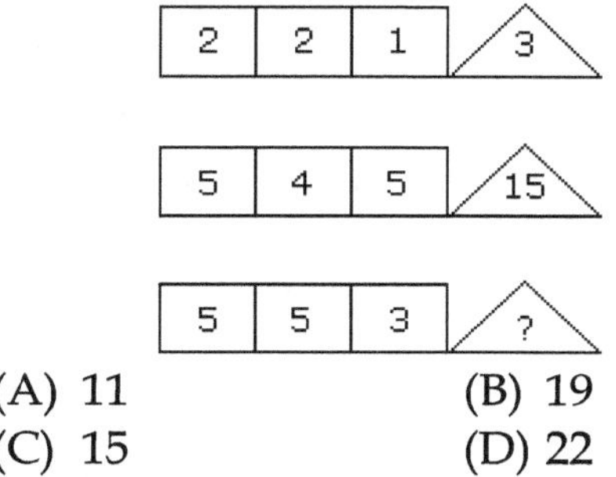

(A) 11   (B) 19
(C) 15   (D) 22

57. Which option will replace the question mark?

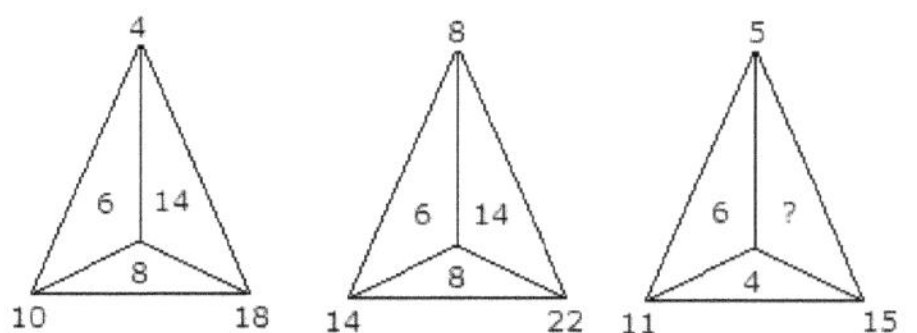

58. Which option will replace the question mark?

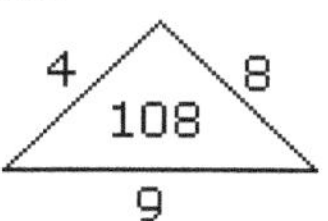 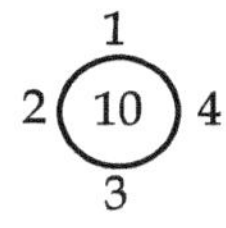 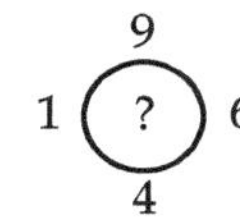

(A) 80   (B) 114
(C) 108   (D) None of these

59. Which option will replace the question mark?

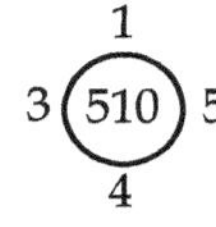 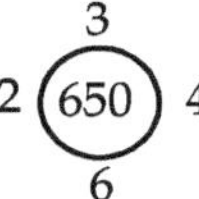 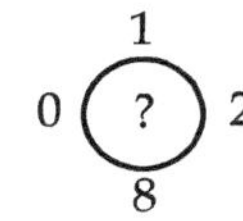

(A) 18   (B) 20
(C) 21   (D) 19

60. Which option will replace the question mark?

$$3\begin{pmatrix}1\\510\\4\end{pmatrix}5 \qquad 2\begin{pmatrix}3\\650\\6\end{pmatrix}4 \qquad 0\begin{pmatrix}1\\?\\8\end{pmatrix}2$$

(A) 660   (B) 670
(C) 610   (D) 690

Top of page options for Q57:

(A) 8   (B) 14
(C) 10   (D) 6

Darken Your Choice with HB Pencil

1.	Ⓐ Ⓑ Ⓒ Ⓓ	13.	Ⓐ Ⓑ Ⓒ Ⓓ	25.	Ⓐ Ⓑ Ⓒ Ⓓ	37	Ⓐ Ⓑ Ⓒ Ⓓ	49.	Ⓐ Ⓑ Ⓒ Ⓓ
2.	Ⓐ Ⓑ Ⓒ Ⓓ	14.	Ⓐ Ⓑ Ⓒ Ⓓ	26.	Ⓐ Ⓑ Ⓒ Ⓓ	38.	Ⓐ Ⓑ Ⓒ Ⓓ	50.	Ⓐ Ⓑ Ⓒ Ⓓ
3.	Ⓐ Ⓑ Ⓒ Ⓓ	15.	Ⓐ Ⓑ Ⓒ Ⓓ	27.	Ⓐ Ⓑ Ⓒ Ⓓ	39.	Ⓐ Ⓑ Ⓒ Ⓓ	51.	Ⓐ Ⓑ Ⓒ Ⓓ
4.	Ⓐ Ⓑ Ⓒ Ⓓ	16.	Ⓐ Ⓑ Ⓒ Ⓓ	28.	Ⓐ Ⓑ Ⓒ Ⓓ	40.	Ⓐ Ⓑ Ⓒ Ⓓ	52.	Ⓐ Ⓑ Ⓒ Ⓓ
5.	Ⓐ Ⓑ Ⓒ Ⓓ	17.	Ⓐ Ⓑ Ⓒ Ⓓ	29.	Ⓐ Ⓑ Ⓒ Ⓓ	41.	Ⓐ Ⓑ Ⓒ Ⓓ	53.	Ⓐ Ⓑ Ⓒ Ⓓ
6.	Ⓐ Ⓑ Ⓒ Ⓓ	18.	Ⓐ Ⓑ Ⓒ Ⓓ	30.	Ⓐ Ⓑ Ⓒ Ⓓ	42.	Ⓐ Ⓑ Ⓒ Ⓓ	54.	Ⓐ Ⓑ Ⓒ Ⓓ
7.	Ⓐ Ⓑ Ⓒ Ⓓ	19.	Ⓐ Ⓑ Ⓒ Ⓓ	31.	Ⓐ Ⓑ Ⓒ Ⓓ	43.	Ⓐ Ⓑ Ⓒ Ⓓ	55.	Ⓐ Ⓑ Ⓒ Ⓓ
8.	Ⓐ Ⓑ Ⓒ Ⓓ	20.	Ⓐ Ⓑ Ⓒ Ⓓ	32.	Ⓐ Ⓑ Ⓒ Ⓓ	44.	Ⓐ Ⓑ Ⓒ Ⓓ	56.	Ⓐ Ⓑ Ⓒ Ⓓ
9.	Ⓐ Ⓑ Ⓒ Ⓓ	21.	Ⓐ Ⓑ Ⓒ Ⓓ	33.	Ⓐ Ⓑ Ⓒ Ⓓ	45.	Ⓐ Ⓑ Ⓒ Ⓓ	57.	Ⓐ Ⓑ Ⓒ Ⓓ
10.	Ⓐ Ⓑ Ⓒ Ⓓ	22.	Ⓐ Ⓑ Ⓒ Ⓓ	34.	Ⓐ Ⓑ Ⓒ Ⓓ	46.	Ⓐ Ⓑ Ⓒ Ⓓ	58.	Ⓐ Ⓑ Ⓒ Ⓓ
11.	Ⓐ Ⓑ Ⓒ Ⓓ	23.	Ⓐ Ⓑ Ⓒ Ⓓ	35.	Ⓐ Ⓑ Ⓒ Ⓓ	47.	Ⓐ Ⓑ Ⓒ Ⓓ	59.	Ⓐ Ⓑ Ⓒ Ⓓ
12.	Ⓐ Ⓑ Ⓒ Ⓓ	24.	Ⓐ Ⓑ Ⓒ Ⓓ	36.	Ⓐ Ⓑ Ⓒ Ⓓ	48.	Ⓐ Ⓑ Ⓒ Ⓓ	60.	Ⓐ Ⓑ Ⓒ Ⓓ

MODEL TEST PAPER

MULTIPLE CHOICE QUESTIONS

1. Find out the alternative figure which contains figure (X) as its part.

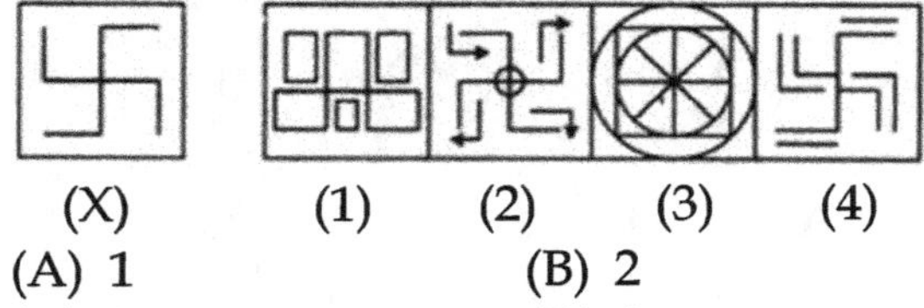

   (X)   (1)   (2)   (3)   (4)

  (A) 1   (B) 2
  (C) 3   (D) 4

2. Solve the given question based on the number series 17 16 14 11 7 ?

  (A) 4   (B) 7
  (C) 3   (D) 2
  (e) None of these

3. A woman introduces a man as the son of the brother of her mother. How is the man related to the woman?

  (A) Son   (B) Nephew
  (C) Grandson   (D) Uncle

4. Rajesh's school bus is facing North when reaches his school. After starting from Rajesh's house, it turning twice and then left before reaching the school. What direction the bus facing when it left the bus stop in front of Rajesh's house?

  (A) East   (B) North
  (C) South   (D) West

5. I am facing South. I turn right and walk 20 m. Then I turn right again and walk 10 m. Then I turn left and walk 10 m and then turning right walk 20 m. Then, I turn right again and walks 60 m. In which direction am I from the starting point?

  (A) North-East   (B) North-West
  (C) North   (D) West

6. Choose the option that represents the correct water image of b r i d g e

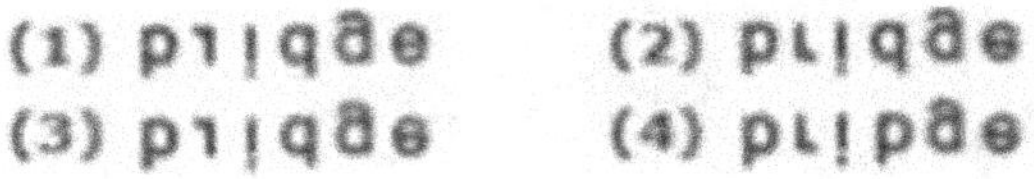

  (1) pᴉᴉqɘ   (2) pᴉᴉqɘ
  (3) pᴉᴉqɘ   (4) pᴉᴉpɘ
  (A) 1   (B) 2
  (C) 3   (D) 4
  (e) None of these

7. Choose the alternative which closely resembles the mirror image of the given combination.

  ANS43Q12

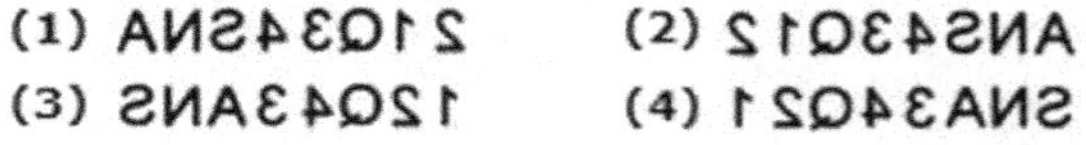

  (1) ANS43Q12 (mirror)   (2) ANS43Q12 (mirror)
  (3) ANS43Q12 (mirror)   (4) ANS43Q12 (mirror)
  (A) 1   (B) 2
  (C) 3   (D) 4

8. Choose the alternative which closely resembles the mirror image of the given combination.

  1965 INDOPAK

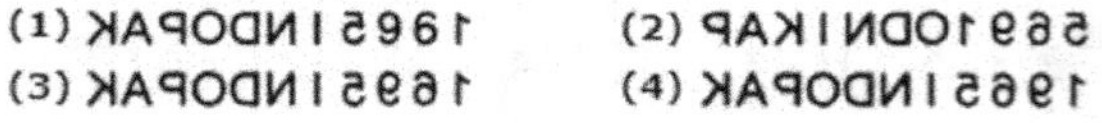

  (1) KAPODNI5691 (mirror)   (2) KAPODNI5691 (mirror)
  (3) KAPODNI5691 (mirror)   (4) KAPODNI5691 (mirror)
  (A) 1   (B) 2
  (C) 3   (D) 4

9. See the analogy and find out the correct option.

  Flow : River :: Stagnant : ?

  (A) Rain   (B) Stream
  (C) Pool   (D) Canal

10. Six friends are sitting in a circle and are facing the centre of the circle. Deepa is between Prakash and Pankaj. Priti is between Mukesh and Lalit. Prakash and

Mukesh are opposite to each other.

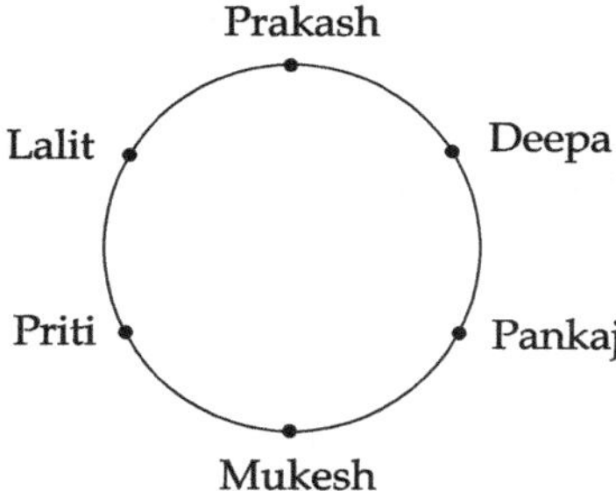

Who is just right to Pankaj?

(A) Deepa   (B) Lalit

(C) Prakash   (D) Priti

11. Which of the following statement(s) about saliva is/are true?

   (A) Saliva helps to digest food

   (B) Saliva causes food to be rolled into a ball

   (C) Saliva moistens the food to make swallowing easier

   (D) Both (A) and (C)

12. Refer the given flowchart and select the correct option.

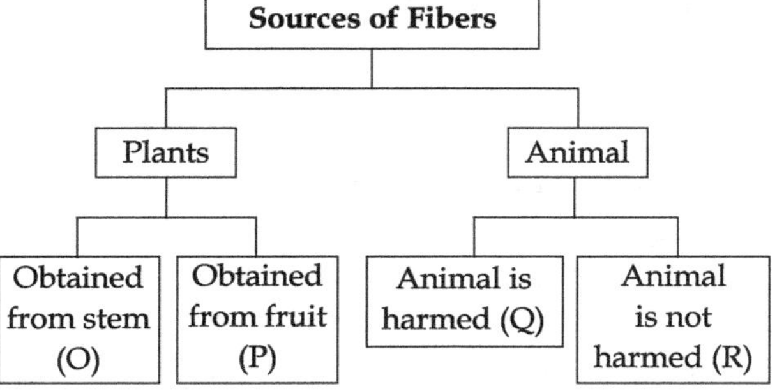

   (A) O: Cotton, P: Flax, Q: Silk, R: Wool

   (B) O: Cotton, P: Flax, Q: Wool, R: Silk

   (C) O: Flax, P: Cotton, Q: Silk, R: Wool

   (D) O: Cotton, P: Silk, Q: Flax, R: Wool

13. Which of these is a correct statement?

   (A) Cotton is also called *Gossypium hirsutum*

   (B) The process of making yarn from raw fibrous material is called spinning

   (C) Jute is a rainy season crop, which grows best in warm, humid climate

   (D) All of them

14. Identify X and Y in the given Venn diagram and select the correct option.

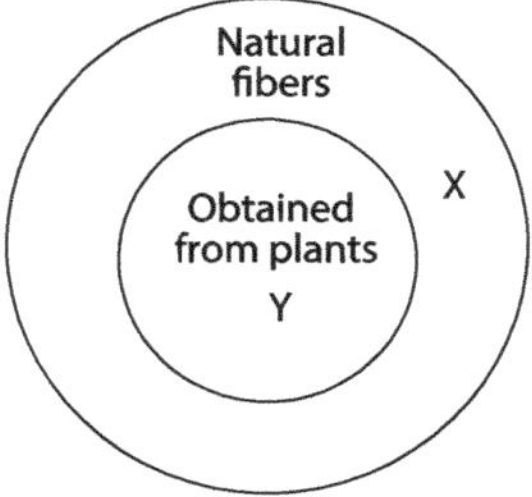

(A) X is nylon   (B) Y is silk

(C) X is rubber   (D) Y is cotton

15. Decantation process is used to separate:

   (A) Two immiscible liquids

   (B) Two miscible liquids

   (C) Two metals in an alloy

   (D) Solid-solid mixture

16. Crude oil is purified using fractional distillation process. This method is based on:

   (A) the difference of the volumes of the components

   (B) the difference of the boiling points of the components

   (C) the difference of the masses of the components

   (D) the difference in the solubility of the components

17. Winnowing isused only for:

   (A) Homogeneous solid-liquid mixture

   (B) Heterogeneous solid-solid mixture

   (C) Homogeneous solid-solid mixture

   (D) Heterogeneous solid-liquid mixture

18. When the temperature of the solid is increased, the _________ energy of the particles increases.

   (A) Heat   (B) Potential

   (C) Kinetic   (D) Chemical

19. Study this Venn diagram.

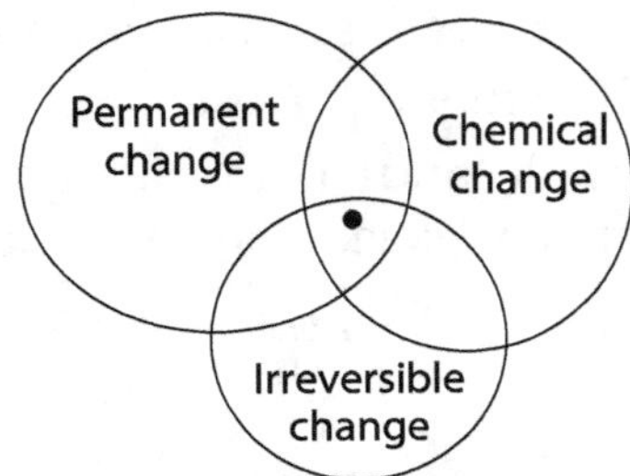

The point at the center represents:

(A) Rusting

(B) Condensation

(C) Melting of ice

(D) Boiling of water

20. What is one common property among the following phenomena?

    1. the rotation of blades of a fan
    2. the blinking of traffic lights
    3. the swinging of a pendulum

    (A) All are periodic changes

    (B) All are irreversible and desirable changes

    (C) All are chemical changes

    (D) All are undesirable changes

21. Shiva covered one of the leaves of his green plant shown below with a piece of black pastel paper. He then kept the plant in a dark place for 2 days.

    After 2 days of darkness, he kept the plant in a bright sunny place for a day. At the end of the day, Shiva conducted an iodine test on the leaf.

    Which one of the diagrams below shows the result of the test?

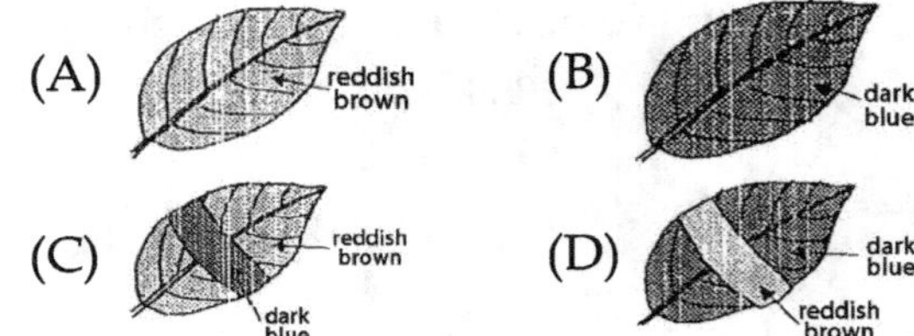

22. Mary made the following statements about photosynthesis.

    Which of the statements is/are incorrect?

    (A) Oxygen production takes place during photosynthesis

    (B) Only heat energy is needed for plants to carry out photosynthesis

    (C) Photosynthesis can only take place in cells that contain chloroplasts

    (D) During respiration, the excess food made during photosynthesis is used up for energy

23. Plants lose gases through __________.

    (A) Flowers

    (B) Seeds

    (C) Small porous roots

    (D) Leaves

24. The smallest time measured by a wrist watch accurately is:

    (A) 60 seconds   (B) 1 second

    (C) 1 hour   (D) 1 millisecond

25. When a drill bores a hole in a piece of wood, it demonstrates:

    (A) Translatory motion

    (B) Rotatory motion

    (C) Translatory and rotatory motion

    (D) Curvilinear motion

26. Two identical metal balls A and B moving in opposite directions hit each other at points X as shown in the figure. Changes are most likely to appear in their:

    (A) Shapes

    (B) Volumes

    (C) Speed

    (D) Speed and direction

27. Adam shone a beam of light from a torch at two objects, X and Y, as shown in the diagram below.

OLYMPIAD WORKBOOK (NSO) CLASS – 6

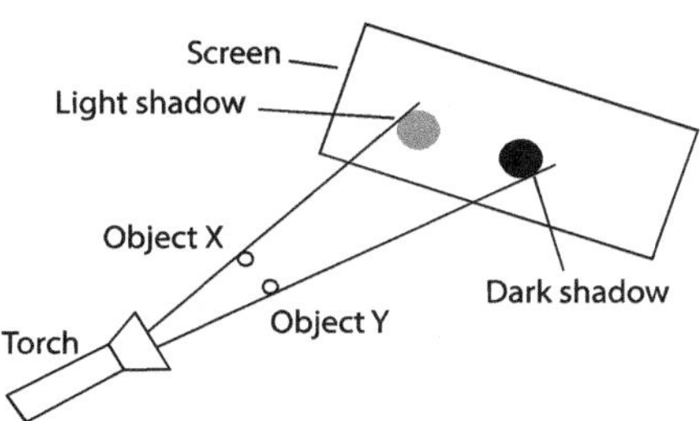

The shadow formed by object X was much lighter than the one formed by object Y.

Which of the following materials are X and Y likely to be made of?

	Object X	Object Y
(A)	Iron	Glass
(B)	Mirror	Paper
(C)	Frosted glass	Copper
(D)	Styrofoam	Tracing paper

28. A plane mirror reflects a pencil of light to form a real image. Then the pencil of light incident on the mirror is _________.
    (A) Divergent   (B) Convergent
    (C) Parallel   (D) None of them

29. Kara performed an experiment. She positioned a tennis ball between a screen and a torch as shown below.

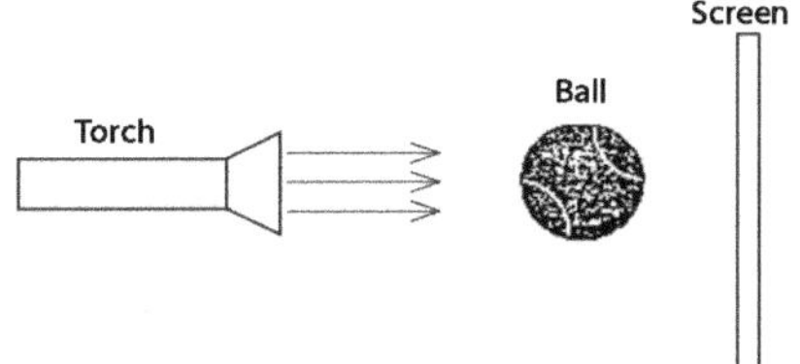

She wrote down the steps she followed:
1. Switch on the torch.
2. Measure the height of the shadow of the tennis ball formed on the screen.
3. Move the tennis ball 5 cm closer to the torch.
4. Measure the height of the shadow again.
5. Repeat steps (3) and (4) twice, moving the tennis ball 5 cm closer to the torch each time.

Which of the following states the correct hypothesis for the above experiment?
(A) The brightness of the torch will affect the size of the shadow
(B) The strength of the battery will affect the darkness of the shadow
(C) The distance between the torch and the tennis ball will affect the height of the shadow
(D) The distance between the tennis ball and the screen will affect the shape of the shadow

30. Sameer's torch does not light up. This could be because of the following reason:
    (A) There is a gap between the batteries
    (B) The metal tip of the bulb is not connected to one of the batteries
    (C) The positive terminal of one battery is not connected to the negative terminal of the next battery
    (D) All are correct

31. Bulb will glow in:

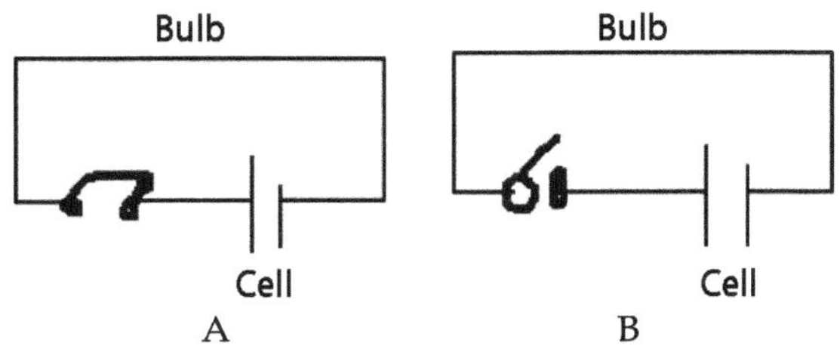

(A) A
(B) B
(C) Both (A) and (B)
(D) None of these

32. In which of the following a permanent magnet not used?
    (A) Loudspeakers
    (B) In magnetic door catches
    (C) In compasses
    (D) None of these

33. The diagram below shows what happens when two objects, X and Y, are placed very close to each other on a piece of paper laced with iron fillings.

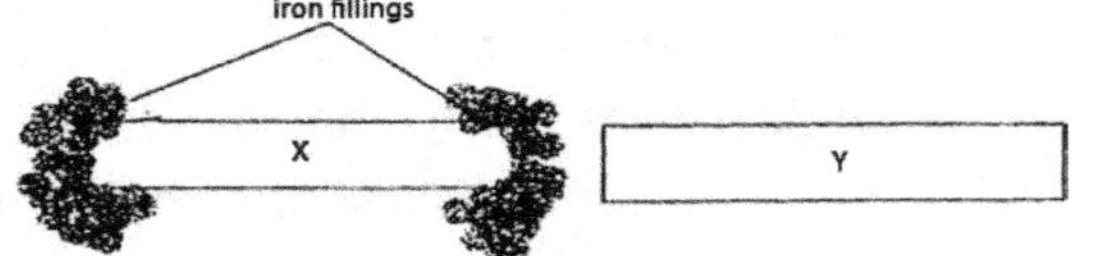

Which one of the following statement(s) is/are definitely true?
(i) Object X is a magnet
(ii) Object X is made of copper
(iii) Object Y is made of non-magnetic material
(iv) Object Y is made of magnetic material
(A) (i) only
(B) (i) and (iii)
(C) (ii) and (iii)
(D) (i), (ii) and (iv)

34. Which of the following groups of items is needed to make an electromagnet?
(A) An iron nail, copper wire and a light bulb
(B) An iron nail, a battery and a light bulb
(C) An iron nail, a battery and a copper wire
(D) None of them

35. The needle of the compass is made of a magnet because it __________.
(A) Attracts metal
(B) Comes to rest in a north-south direction
(C) Gets deflected when a magnet is brought closer
(D) Both (B) and (C)

36. Four nails of different materials – iron, steel, copper, aluminum – were stroked with a magnet. Which of them will turn into a magnet?
(A) Iron and steel nails
(B) Iron and copper nails
(C) Iron and aluminum nails
(D) All of these

37. Set-ups A and B below are placed on a table in the science room.

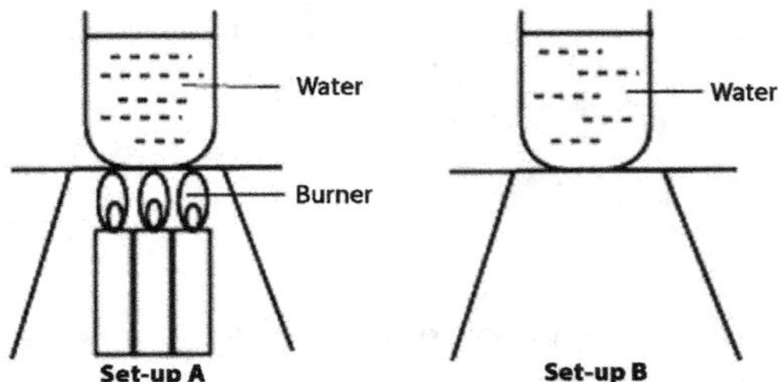

What are the similarities that can be observed in both set-ups after 45 minutes?
(A) The volume of water decreases
(B) The temperature of the water increases
(C) The water gains heat and evaporates
(D) Both (A) and (C)

38. Which of the following situations show(s) that heat is lost?
(i) When ice melts
(ii) When water vapour condenses
(iii) When water changes to ice
(iv) When a steel pot is left in the fridge
(A) (i) and (ii)
(B) (ii) only
(C) (ii), (iii) and (iv)
(D) (iii) and (iv)

39. Early in the morning, Ryan observed that there were water droplets on the outside of cars, even though it did not rain the night before.

What is the correct explanation for Ryan observation?
(A) Water vapour on the cool car condensed into the air
(B) Water droplets from the warm air evaporated on the car
(C) Water vapour from the air condensed on the cool car
(D) Water droplets on the warm car evaporated to the air

40. Read the following statements about diseases.
(i) They are caused by germs
(ii) They are caused due to lack of nutrients in our diet

OLYMPIAD WORKBOOK (NSO) CLASS– 6

(iii) They can be passed on to another person through contact

(iv) They can be prevented by taking a balanced diet

Which pair of statements best describes a deficiency disease?

(A) (i) and (ii)
(B) (ii) and (iv)
(C) (i) only
(D) (i), (ii) and (iii)

41. **Direction:** Question is based on the following flow chart which gives the techniques a student adopted to separate the constituents of a mixture.

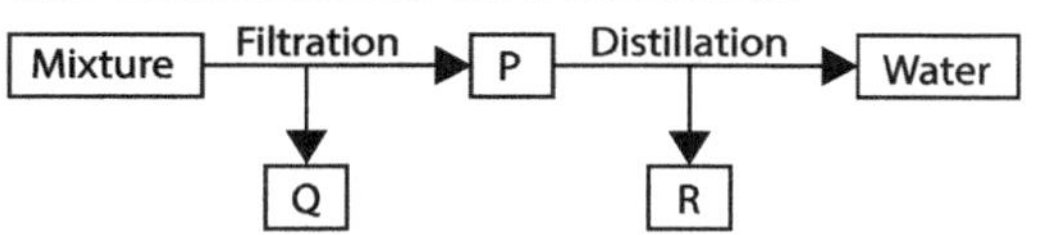

What could substance R be?

(A) Sugar
(B) Chalk powder
(C) Glass
(D) Oxygen

42. **Direction:** Question is based on the following flow chart which gives the techniques a student adopted to separate the constituents of a mixture.

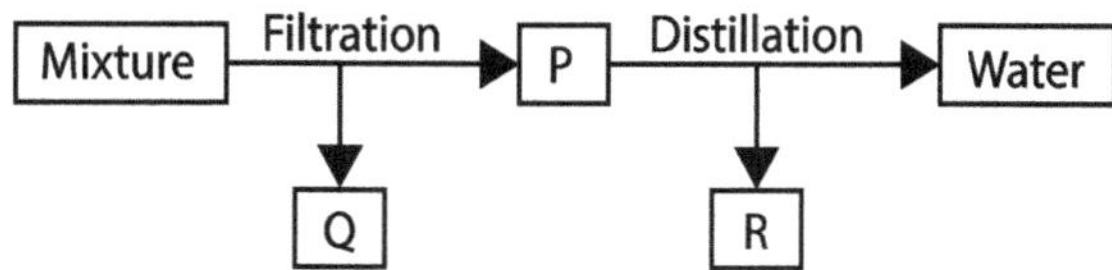

What is substance Q?

(A) Sugar
(B) Chalk powder
(C) Alcohol
(D) Oxygen

43. Observe the given diagram carefully and fill in the blanks.

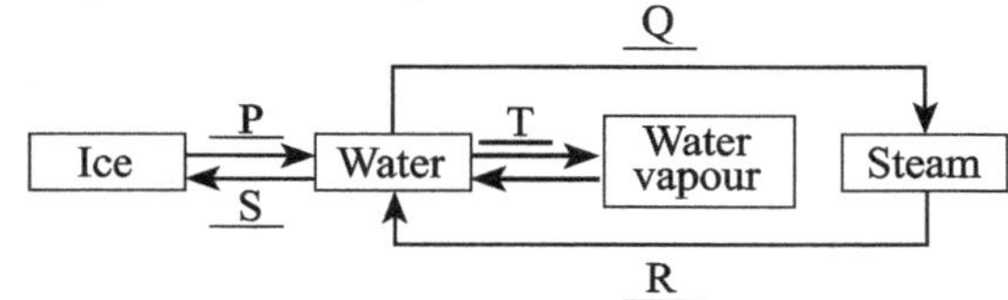

	P	Q	R	S	T
(A)	Freezing	Boiling	Condensation	Melting	Evaporation
(B)	Freezing	Evaporation	Boiling	Melting	Condensation
(C)	Melting	Boiling	Condensation	Freezing	Evaporation
(D)	Melting	Evaporation	Condensation	Freezing	Boiling

44. Read the given passage.

Animals X, Y and Z are found in completely different habitats. Animal X is nocturnal and has developed many characters to conserve as much water as possible in the body. Animal Y has furry body with thick skin. It is large in size and has padded feet. Animal Z is adapted to live on trees, sticky pads on its feet help it to climb trees.

Which of the following can you conclude regarding the habitats of these animals?

(A) Animal X lives in a place with annual rainfall of about 80-100 cm.

(B) Animal Y lives in a place where days may be extremely hot and nights can be very cold.

(C) Animal Z lives in an area with annual rainfall of about 20-25 cm.

(D) Animal Y lives in an area where temperature sometimes reach 0°C or fall below it.

45. Which of the following graphs correctly shows the change in volume with temperature of water?

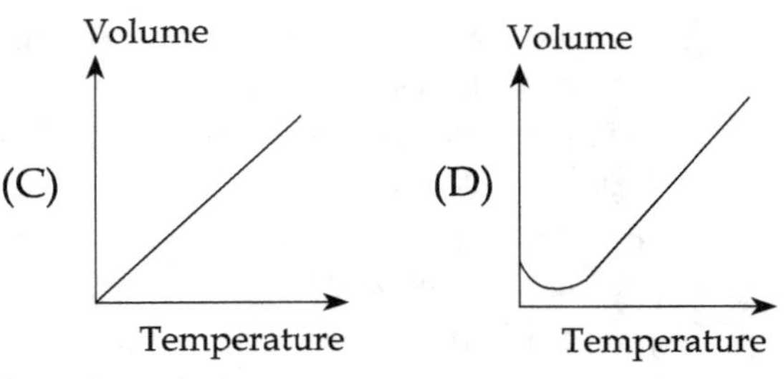

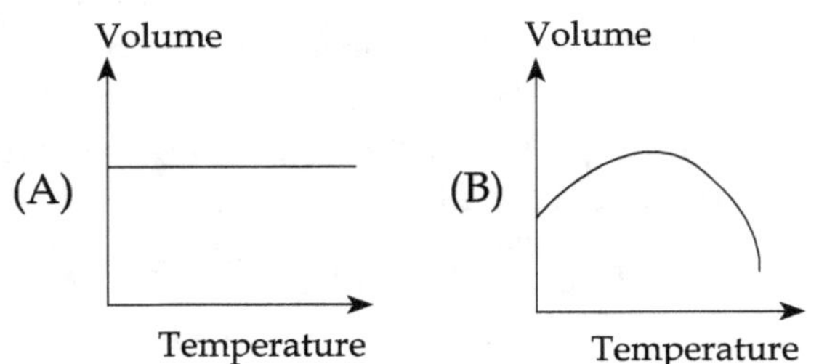

(A), (B), (C), (D) graphs of Volume vs Temperature.

46. Understand the classification shown below and choose the correct option that follow.

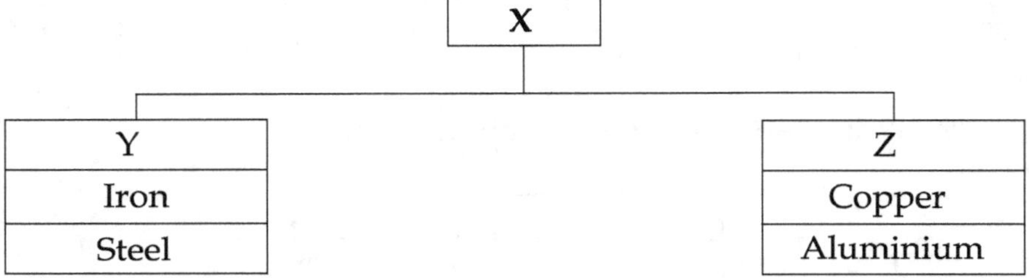

Which of the following correctly describes the X, Y and Z?

	X	Y	Z
(A)	Metals	Can sink	Can float
(B)	Metals	Can be magnetized	Cannot magnetized
(C)	Metals	Can be attached by magnets	Cannot be attached by magnets
(D)	Metals	Can allow electricity to pass through	Cannot allow electricity to pass through

47. The diagram below shows a floating plant, the water hyacinth, and its parts labelled A, B, C and D.

Sanya has started to point out the functions of the parts as follows.

Parts	Functions
P	Helps in photosynthesis
Q	Traps light to make food
R	Helps the plant to float on water
S	Holds the plant firmly to the soil

Which part(s) of the plant is wrongly matched to its functions?

(A) R only
(B) P only
(C) P and Q only
(D) Q and S only

48. When a drill bores a hole into a piece of wood, it describes:
   (i)   Oscillatory motion
   (ii) Rotatory motion
   (iii) Curvilinear motion
   (iv) Translatory motion
   (A) (i) and (ii)   (B) (ii) and (iii)
   (C) (i) and (iv)   (D) ii and (iv)

49. In an experiment, two set-ups are created. In the Set-up X, the salt has been added to the ice while in the Set-up Y, only ice cubes were added.

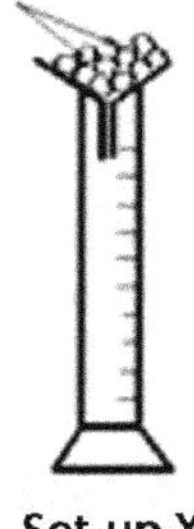
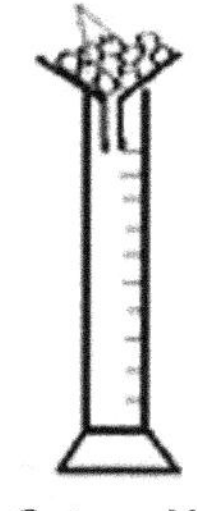

Which of the following statement(s) is correct for the experiment described above? Choose the correct option to answer the question.
   (i)   Salt decreases the melting temperature of ice below −20°C.
   (ii) Ice in Set-up X melts slower than the ice in Set-up Y.
   (iii) More water will be collected in Set-up X than that in Set-up Y.
   (iv) The water collected from Set-up Y will take longer time to freeze than the water collected from Set-up X.
   (A) (i) only
   (B) (i) and (ii) only
   (C) (i), (ii) and (iii) only
   (D) (ii), (iii) and (iv) only

50. The diagram below shows four circuits with different arrangements of identical batteries and identical bulbs. The bulbs in all four circuits light up.

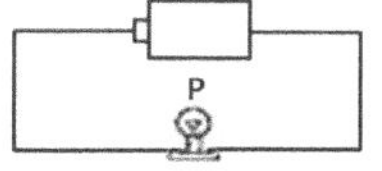
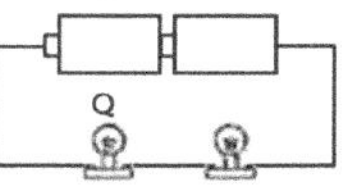
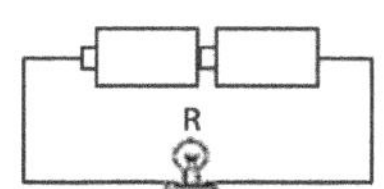
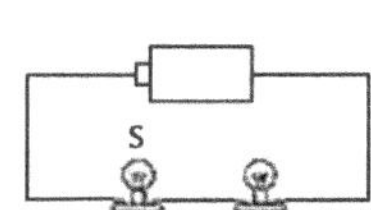

Which of the following pairs of bulbs have the same brightness? Choose the correct option.
   (A) P and Q   (B) P and S
   (C) Q and R   (D) R and S

—Darken Your Choice with HB Pencil—

1. Ⓐ Ⓑ Ⓒ Ⓓ	11. Ⓐ Ⓑ Ⓒ Ⓓ	21. Ⓐ Ⓑ Ⓒ Ⓓ	31 Ⓐ Ⓑ Ⓒ Ⓓ	41. Ⓐ Ⓑ Ⓒ Ⓓ
2. Ⓐ Ⓑ Ⓒ Ⓓ	12. Ⓐ Ⓑ Ⓒ Ⓓ	22. Ⓐ Ⓑ Ⓒ Ⓓ	32. Ⓐ Ⓑ Ⓒ Ⓓ	42. Ⓐ Ⓑ Ⓒ Ⓓ
3. Ⓐ Ⓑ Ⓒ Ⓓ	13. Ⓐ Ⓑ Ⓒ Ⓓ	23. Ⓐ Ⓑ Ⓒ Ⓓ	33. Ⓐ Ⓑ Ⓒ Ⓓ	43. Ⓐ Ⓑ Ⓒ Ⓓ
4. Ⓐ Ⓑ Ⓒ Ⓓ	14. Ⓐ Ⓑ Ⓒ Ⓓ	24. Ⓐ Ⓑ Ⓒ Ⓓ	34. Ⓐ Ⓑ Ⓒ Ⓓ	44. Ⓐ Ⓑ Ⓒ Ⓓ
5. Ⓐ Ⓑ Ⓒ Ⓓ	15. Ⓐ Ⓑ Ⓒ Ⓓ	25. Ⓐ Ⓑ Ⓒ Ⓓ	35. Ⓐ Ⓑ Ⓒ Ⓓ	45. Ⓐ Ⓑ Ⓒ Ⓓ
6. Ⓐ Ⓑ Ⓒ Ⓓ	16. Ⓐ Ⓑ Ⓒ Ⓓ	26. Ⓐ Ⓑ Ⓒ Ⓓ	36. Ⓐ Ⓑ Ⓒ Ⓓ	46. Ⓐ Ⓑ Ⓒ Ⓓ
7. Ⓐ Ⓑ Ⓒ Ⓓ	17. Ⓐ Ⓑ Ⓒ Ⓓ	27. Ⓐ Ⓑ Ⓒ Ⓓ	37. Ⓐ Ⓑ Ⓒ Ⓓ	47. Ⓐ Ⓑ Ⓒ Ⓓ
8. Ⓐ Ⓑ Ⓒ Ⓓ	18. Ⓐ Ⓑ Ⓒ Ⓓ	28. Ⓐ Ⓑ Ⓒ Ⓓ	38. Ⓐ Ⓑ Ⓒ Ⓓ	48. Ⓐ Ⓑ Ⓒ Ⓓ
9. Ⓐ Ⓑ Ⓒ Ⓓ	19. Ⓐ Ⓑ Ⓒ Ⓓ	29. Ⓐ Ⓑ Ⓒ Ⓓ	39. Ⓐ Ⓑ Ⓒ Ⓓ	49. Ⓐ Ⓑ Ⓒ Ⓓ
10. Ⓐ Ⓑ Ⓒ Ⓓ	20. Ⓐ Ⓑ Ⓒ Ⓓ	30. Ⓐ Ⓑ Ⓒ Ⓓ	40. Ⓐ Ⓑ Ⓒ Ⓓ	50. Ⓐ Ⓑ Ⓒ Ⓓ

HINTS AND SOLUTIONS

1. FOOD, HEALTH AND HYGIENE

Answer Key

1. (C)	2. (C)	3. (B)	4. (B)	5. (A)	6. (C)	7. (B)	8. (A)	9. (B)	10. (C)
11. (C)	12. (A)	13. (C)	14. (C)	15. (B)	16. (C)	17. (D)	18. (D)	19. (B)	20. (B)
21. (B)	22. (C)	23. (A)	24. (B)	25. (B)	26. (D)	27. (A)	28. (C)	29. (B)	30. (B)

HOTS (ACHIEVERS SECTION)

31. (B)	32. (B)	33. (A)	34. (C)	35. (B)

2. FIBER TO FABRIC

Answer Key

1. (A)	2. (D)	3. (D)	4. (C)	5. (D)	6. (A)	7. (D)	8. (A)	9. (A)	10. (C)
11. (A)	12. (A)	13. (A)	14. (C)	15. (C)	16. (A)	17. (D)	18. (A)	19. (B)	20. (C)
21. (A)	22. (D)	23. (D)	24. (C)	25. (B)	26. (A)	27. (D)	28. (B)	29. (C)	30. (C)

HOTS (ACHIEVERS SECTION)

31. (D)	32. (C)	33. (C)	34. (B)	35. (C)

3. SORTING AND SEPARATION OF MATERIALS

Answer Key

1. (C)	2. (B)	3. (D)	4. (B)	5. (C)	6. (D)	7. (B)	8. (B)	9. (D)	10. (B)
11. (A)	12. (C)	13. (D)	14. (B)	15. (D)	16. (B)	17. (B)	18. (B)	19. (D)	20. (B)
21. (C)	22. (D)	23. (D)	24. (C)	25. (C)	26. (B)	27. (C)	28. (A).	29. (B)	30. (A)

HOTS (ACHIEVERS SECTION)

31. (A)	32. (C)	33. (D)	34. (A)	35. (D)

4. CHANGES AROUND US

Answer Key

1. (A)	2. (B)	3. (D)	4. (A)	5. (A)	6. (A)	7. (C)	8. (D)	9. (D)	10. (B)
11. (C)	12. (B)	13. (A)	14. (D)	15. (C)	16. (B)	17. (C)	18. (B)	19. (C)	20. (C)
21. (C)	22. (C)	23. (A)	24. (D)	25. (B)	26. (B)	27. (A)	28. (B)	29. (C)	30. (D)

HOTS (ACHIEVERS SECTION)

31. (D)	32. (C)	33. (C)	34. (C)	35. (B)

5. LIVING ORGANISMS AND THEIR SURROUNDINGS

Answer Key

1. (A)	2. (C)	3. (D)	4. (D)	5. (D)	6. (C)	7. (D)	8. (D)	9. (B)	10. (C)
11. (A)	12. (C)	13. (C)	14. (C)	15. (B)	16. (B)	17. (B)	18. (B)	19. (B)	20. (A)
21. (B)	22. (D)	23. (A)	24. (B)	25. (D)	26. (D)	27. (C)	28. (C)	29. (A)	30. (C)

HOTS (ACHIEVERS SECTION)

31. (A)	32. (A)	33. (C)	34. (C)	35. (D)

6. MOTION AND MEASUREMENT OF DISTANCES

Answer Key

1. (A)	2. (B)	3. (A)	4. (D)	5. (B)	6. (C)	7. (D)	8. (C)	9. (C)	10. (D)
11. (D)	12. (C)	13. (A)	14. (C)	15. (B)	16. (B)	17. (D)	18. (D)	19. (A)	20. (B)
21. (C)	22. (A)	23. (D)	24. (B)	25. (C)					

11. (D)

If Kavya takes 10 minutes to cover 2 km, then in 1 minute, she will cover 2 km ÷ 10 = 0.2 km (using the formula: speed = distance travelled ÷ time taken) Similarly, if Yamini takes 20 minutes to cover 5 km, then in 1 minute she will cover 5 km ÷ 20 = 0.25 km.

HOTS (ACHIEVERS SECTION)

26. (B)	27. (A)	28. (D)	29. (C)	30. (A)

7. LIGHT, SHADOWS AND REFLECTION

Answer Key

1. (C)	2. (B)	3. (B)	4. (C)	5. (C)	6. (B)	7. (B)	8. (D)	9. (C)	10. (B)
11. (A)	12. (B)	13. (A)	14. (C)	15. (A)	16. (D)	17. (A)	18. (C)	19. (B)	20. (C)
21. (D)	22. (B)	23. (C)	24. (D)	25. (D)	26. (C)	27. (B)	28. (A)	29. (B)	30. (A)

HOTS (ACHIEVERS SECTION)

31. (B)	32. (D)	33. (B)	34. (C)	35. (C)

8. ELECTRICITY AND CIRCUITS

Answer Key

1. (B)	2. (D)	3. (A)	4. (D)	5. (B)	6. (C)	7. (D)	8. (A)	9. (B)	10. (A)
11. (C)	12. (A)	13. (A)	14. (B)	15. (C)	16. (C)	17. (B)	18. (D)	19. (B)	20. (A)
21. (D)	22. (D)	23. (B)	24. (D)	25. (D)	26. (D)	27. (A)	28. (B)	29. (C)	30. (B)

HOTS (ACHIEVERS SECTION)

31. (C)	32. (C)	33. (B)	34. (A)	35. (A)

Answer Key

1. (C)	2. (A)	3. (B)	4. (D)	5. (D)	6. (C)	7. (A)	8. (D)	9. (A)	10. (C)
11. (A)	12. (C)	13. (B)	14. (A)	15. (B)	16. (C)	17. (A)	18. (B)	19. (B)	20. (C)
21. (B)	22. (C)	23. (C)	24. (D)	25. (C)	26. (D)	27. (C)	28. (C)	29. (D)	30. (C)

HOTS (ACHIEVERS SECTION)

31. (D)	32. (A)	33. (D)	34. (D)	35. (D)

10. OUR ENVIRONMENT

Answer Key

1. (D)	2. (B)	3. (B)	4. (A)	5. (A)	6. (D)	7. (C)	8. (B)	9. (A)	10. (B)
11. (C)	12. (A)	13. (B)	14. (D)	15. (A)	16. (A)	17. (B)	18. (C)	19. (B)	20. (D)

1. **(D)**
   Frogs usually have ponds as their habitat not the oceans.

2. **(B)**
   Animals living deep in the ocean do not have streamlined shape. However, when they move in water they make their body shapes streamlined. They also do not have blowholes and strong hind limbs.

3. **(B)**
   Deer do not have eyes in the front, It has eyes on the side of its head allow it to look in all directions for danger.

4. **(A)**
   Bats have an aerial habitat. They are the only mammals capable of true flight.

6. **(D)**
   Abiotic components are non-living chemical and physical parts of the environment that affect living organisms and the functioning of ecosystems, e.g. soil, rain, wind, temperature, pH, and sunlight etc.

8. **(B)**
   Grass is an autotroph and a plant. Most plants are autotrophs because they make their own food. Some plant species are parasitic, meaning they get their nutrients from other sources. Parasitic plants are heterotrophic.

9. **(A)**
   Herbivores are animals that feeds on plants, e.g. rabbit.

10. (B)

An autotroph or producer, is an organism that produces complex organic compounds from simple substances present in its surroundings, generally using energy from light or inorganic chemical reactions.

11. (C)

The organisms that feed on both plant and animal products are known as omnivorous.

12. (A)

Examples of decomposers include bacteria, fungi, some insects, and snails.

13. (B)

Tiger is present at the top of the trophic level.

14. (D)

Grass (producer) → Rat (omnivore) → Snake (bigger carnivore) → Eagle (top carnivore)

15. (A)

Plants are called producers. This is because they produce their own food.

16. (A)

Among the given options, cockroach is the only omnivorous animal. Cockroaches feed on decaying matter.

18. (C)

Humans are omnivores as they eat both plants and animals.

20. (D)

Among the given options, an aquarium is the best example of a mini ecosystem.

HOTS (ACHIEVERS SECTION)

21. (C)	22. (D)	23. (B)	24. (C)	25. (C)

21. (C)

Leaves are modified into spines in A, so it probably belong to the desert habitat where there is very less rainfall. Plants in desert habitat have deep roots to absorb water.

22. (D)

An aquatic bird will have both webbed feet and hollow bones. Webbed feet will help it swim and hollow bones are required for light weight in flying.

23. (B)

Submerged plants have ribbon like or highly divided leaves through which the water can easily flow without damaging them, thus by seeing the leaves it could be concluded that it is a submerged plant.

24. (C)

The 3 sentences respectively signifies growth, breathing and excretion. Chicken grows and becomes hen, Abdomen moves while resting due to breathing and we get rid of wastes in the process of excretion.

25. (C)

Photosynthesis produces more oxygen compared to its utilisation by process of respiration and occurs during the day, whereas process of respiration occurs all 24 hours.

Answer Key

1. (C)	2. (A)	3. (C)	4. (B)	5. (A)	6. (B)	7. (C)	8. (C)	9. (C)	10. (D)
11. (B)	12. (B)	13. (D)	14. (C)	15. (A)	16. (B)	17. (C)	18. (A)	19. (B)	20. (A)
21. (D)	22. (C)	23. (A)	24. (A)	25. (C)	26. (C)	27. (B)	28. (B)	29. (A)	30. (D)
31. (C)	32. (A)	33. (C)	34. (C)	35. (C)	36. (B)	37. (D)	38. (C)	39. (A)	40. (A)
41. (D)	42. (D)	43. (C)	44. (D)	45. (D)	46. (C)	47. (D)	48. (B)	49. (D)	50. (A)
51. (D)	52. (A)	53. (D)	54. (C)	55. (B)	56. (D)	57. (C)	58. (C)	59. (B)	60. (D)

1. **(C)**
   From fig (i) $(112 \div 14) \times 2 = 16$
   From fig (ii) $(168 \div 24) \times 2 = 14$
   From fig (iii) $(144 \div 16) \times 2 = 9 \times 2 = 18$

2. **(A)**
   From fig (i) $4 \times 6 + 18 \times 3 = 24 + 54 = 78$
   From fig (ii) $3 \times 5 + 24 \times 4 = 15 + 96 = 111$
   From fig (iii) $2 \times 7 + 21 \times 4 = 14 + 84 = 98$

3. **(C)**
   From fig (i) $1 + 2 = 3 \to 3^2 = 9$
   From fig (ii) $3 + 4 = 7 \to 7^2 = 49$
   $5 + 4 = 9 \to 9^2 = 81$
   $7 + 6 = 13 \to 13^2 = 169$

4. **(B)**
   From fig (i) $2^2 \times 3^2 = 4 \times 9 = 36$
   From fig (ii) $4^2 \times 5^2 = 16 \times 25 = 400$
   From fig (iii) $6^2 \times 7^2 = 36 \times 49 = 1764$

5. **(A)**
   From fig (i) $(14 + 24) - 2 = 38 - 2 = 36$
   From fig (ii) $(23 + 35) - 3 = 58 - 3 = 55$
   From fig (iii) $(34 + 45) - 4 = 79 - 4 = 75$

6. **(B)**
   As Physician does the treatment, similarly Judge delivers the judgement.

7. **(C)**
   As effect of Ice is coldness, similarly the effect of Earth is gravitation.

8. **(C)**
   As the result of Race is Fatigue, similarly the result of Fast is Hunger.

9. **(C)**
   As opposite meaning of peace is chaos, similarly, opposite meaning of creation is destruction.

10. **(D)**
    As Tiger is found in Forest, similarly Otter is found in the water.

11. **(B)**
    The given series is

    $$67 \quad 74 \quad 81 \quad 88 \quad 95 \quad 102$$
    $$+7 \quad +7 \quad +7 \quad +7 \quad +7$$

12. **(B)**

The given series is

109	101	94	88	83	79

$$-8 \quad -7 \quad -6 \quad -5 \quad -4$$

13. **(D)**

The given series is

9	25	49	81	121	169

$$3^2 \quad 5^2 \quad 7^2 \quad 9^2 \quad 11^2 \quad 13^2$$

14. **(C)**

The given series is

3	8	15	24	35	48	63	80

$$(2^2 - 1) \quad (3^2 - 1) \quad (4^2 - 1) \quad (5^2 - 1) \quad (6^2 - 1) \quad (7^2 - 1) \quad (8^2 - 1) \quad (9^2 - 1)$$

15. **(A)**

The given series is

6	12	24	48	96	192	384

$$\times 2 \quad \times 2 \quad \times 2 \quad \times 2 \quad \times 2 \quad \times 2$$

19. **(B)**

All except marble are precious stones.

20. **(A)**

All except peel are different form of cooking.

21. **(D)**

Each letter of the word 'TRUTH' is replaced by a set of two letters – one preceding it and the other following it – in the code. Thus, T is replaced by SU, R is replaced by QS and so on.

22. **(C)**

All the letters of the word, except the last letter, are written in a reverse order to obtain the code.

23. **(A)**

Here,

$$\text{SILVER} \rightarrow \text{SIL/VER} \xrightarrow{\text{Reversing}} \text{LIS/REV}$$
$$\xrightarrow{+1} \text{MJT/SFW}$$

24. **(A)**

Divide the given word into six sets of two letters each and label these sets from 1 to 6. Then the code contains these sets in the order 4, 3, 5, 2, 6, 1 with the letters of sets 3, 2, 1 written in a reverse order. Thus, we have:

$$\underset{1}{\text{VI}} \; \underset{2}{\text{SH}} \; \underset{3}{\text{WA}} \; \underset{4}{\text{NA}} \; \underset{5}{\text{TH}} \; \underset{6}{\text{AN}} \rightarrow \underset{4}{\text{NA}} \; \underset{3}{\text{AW}} \; \underset{5}{\text{TH}} \; \underset{2}{\text{HS}} \; \underset{6}{\text{AN}} \; \underset{1}{\text{IV}}$$

25. **(C)**

Divide the word into three groups of two letters each and write the letters of each group in the reverse order.

$$\text{AN SW ER} \rightarrow \text{NA WS RE} \rightarrow \text{NBWTRF}$$

26. **(C)**

Groan, Grotesque, Group, Guarantee.

27. **(B)**

Nature, Nautical, Naval, Necessary.

28. **(B)**

Foetus, Foliage, Foment, Forceps.

29. **(A)**

Deuce, Devise, Dew, Dexterity.

30. **(D)**

Qualify, Quarrel, Quarry, Quarter.

31. (C)

The given series is

2 8 4 3 8 5 4 8 2 6 7 8 4 6 2 8 4 1 7

33. (C)

The given series is

7 4 5 7 6 8 4 2 1 3 5 1 7 6 8 9 2

34. (C)

The given series is

5 9 3 1 7 4 5 8 4 6 7 4 3 1 4 7 4 2 8 7 4 1

35. (C)

The given series is

4 3 5 6 4 5 2 3 4 5 8 5 4 6 7 5 2 6 9 8 5 1 2 4 5

36. (B)

Sun rises in the east in the morning. So, in morning, the shadow falls towards the west. Now, Mohan's shadow falls to his right. So, he is standing, facing south.

37. (D)

In diagram (A) the directions are shown as they actually are. Diagram (B) is as per the given data. So, comparing the direction of north in (A) with that in (B), north will be called north west.

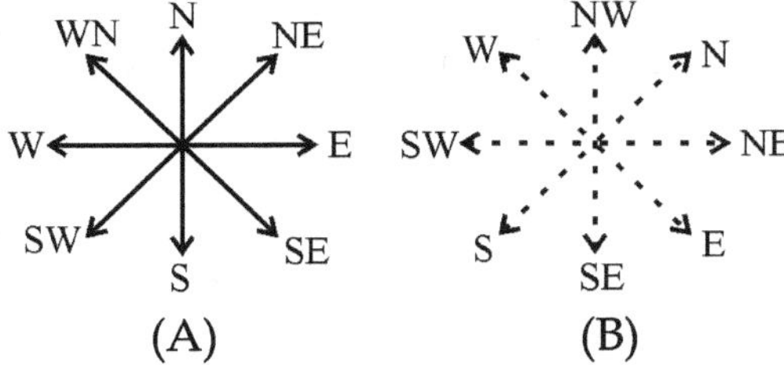

38. (C)

As per the given data, C faces north. A faces towards west. D is to the right of C. So, D is facing towards south. Thus, B who is the partner of D will face towards north.

39. (A)

It is clear from the adjoining diagram that Rakesh lies to the east of Rajesh.

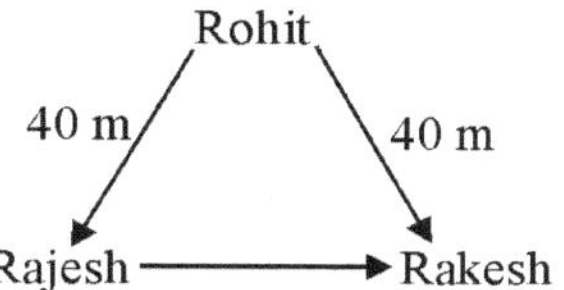

40. (A)

Starting from his house in the East, Pravin moves west wards. Then, the theatre, which is the left, will be in the south. The hospital, which is straight ahead, will be to the west. So, the college will be to the north.

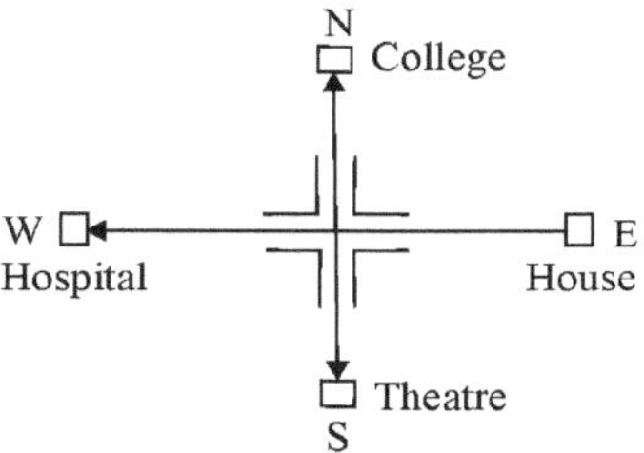

41. (D)

Knowledge is gained through experience or study, so learning is the essential element. A school (choice a) is not necessary for learning or knowledge to take place, nor is a teacher or a textbook (choices b and c).

42. (D)

A culture is the behaviour pattern of a particular population, so customs are the essential element. A culture may or may not be civil or educated (choices a and b). A culture may be an agricultural society (choice c), but this is not the essential element.

43. (C)

An antique is something that belongs to, or was made in, an earlier period. It may or may not be a rarity (choice a), and it cannot be an artifact, an object produced or shaped by human craft (choice b). An antique is old but does not have to be prehistoric (choice d).

44. (D)

A dimension is a measure of spatial content. A compass (choice a) and ruler (choice b) may help determine the dimension, but other instruments may also be used, so these are not the essential element here. An inch (choice c) is only one way to determine a dimension.

45. (D)

A purchase is an acquisition of something. A purchase may be made by trade (choice a) or with money (choice b), so those are not essential elements. A bank (choice c) may or may not be involved in a purchase.

56. (D)

From figure I $(2 \times 2 - 1) = 3$

and from figure II $(5 \times 4 - 5) = 15$

From figure III $(5 \times 5 - 3) = 22$

57. (C)

For first triangle,

$10 - 4 = 6$

$18 - 10 = 8$

$18 - 4 = 14$

For second triangle,

$14 - 8 = 6$

$22 - 14 = 8$

$22 - 8 = 14$

For third triangle,

$11 - 5 = 6$

$15 - 11 = 4$

$\therefore ? = 15 - 5 = 10$

58. (C)

From figure I $(4 + 8) \times 9 = 108$

$\therefore ? = (5 + 4) \times 12 = 108$

59. (B)

$1 + 2 + 3 + 4 = 10$

and $1 + 3 + 5 + 8 = 17$

Similarly, $? = 1 + 4 + 6 + 9 = 20$

60. (D)

From figure I $(1)^2 + (5)^2 + (4)^2 + (3)^2$

$\qquad = 51 \times 10 = 510$

and from figure II $(3)^2 + (4)^2 + (6)^2 + (2)^2$

$\qquad = 65 \times 10 = 650$

Similarly, from figure III $(0)^2 + (1)^2 + (2)^2 + (8)^2 = 69 \times 10 = 690$

MODEL TEST PAPER

Answer Key

1. (C)	2. (D)	3. (D)	4. (D)	5. (A)	6. (B)	7. (B)	8. (D)	9. (C)	10. (A)
11. (D)	12. (C)	13. (D)	14. (D)	15. (A)	16. (B)	17. (B)	18. (C)	19. (A)	20. (A)
21. (D)	22. (B)	23. (D)	24. (B)	25. (C)	26. (D)	27. (C)	28. (B)	29. (C)	30. (D)
31. (A)	32. (D)	33. (B)	34. (C)	35. (D)	36. (A)	37. (A)	38. (C)	39. (C)	40. (B)
41. (A)	42. (B)	43. (C)	44. (D)	45. (D)	46. (B)	47. (B)	48. (D)	49. (B)	50. (A)

SAMPLE OMR ANSWER SHEET

1. STUDENT NAME (IN ENGLISH CAPITAL LETTERS ONLY)

Students must write and darken the respective circles completely using HB Pencil only. Othewise their Answer Sheets will not be evaluated.

PERSONAL DETAILS

2. SCHOOL CODE

3. CLASS

4. SECTION

5. ROLL NO.

6. QUESTION PAPER SET

A ○
B ○
C ○
D ○

7. MOBILE NUMBER

8. GENDER

MALE ○

FEMALE ○

9. STREAM
(Only for Class XI and XII Students)

MATHEMATICS ○
BIOLOGY ○
OTHERS ○

MARK YOUR ANSWERS

No.	A	B	C	D	No.	A	B	C	D
1.	Ⓐ	Ⓑ	Ⓒ	Ⓓ	26.	Ⓐ	Ⓑ	Ⓒ	Ⓓ
2.	Ⓐ	Ⓑ	Ⓒ	Ⓓ	27.	Ⓐ	Ⓑ	Ⓒ	Ⓓ
3.	Ⓐ	Ⓑ	Ⓒ	Ⓓ	28.	Ⓐ	Ⓑ	Ⓒ	Ⓓ
4.	Ⓐ	Ⓑ	Ⓒ	Ⓓ	29.	Ⓐ	Ⓑ	Ⓒ	Ⓓ
5.	Ⓐ	Ⓑ	Ⓒ	Ⓓ	30.	Ⓐ	Ⓑ	Ⓒ	Ⓓ
6.	Ⓐ	Ⓑ	Ⓒ	Ⓓ	31.	Ⓐ	Ⓑ	Ⓒ	Ⓓ
7.	Ⓐ	Ⓑ	Ⓒ	Ⓓ	32.	Ⓐ	Ⓑ	Ⓒ	Ⓓ
8.	Ⓐ	Ⓑ	Ⓒ	Ⓓ	33.	Ⓐ	Ⓑ	Ⓒ	Ⓓ
9.	Ⓐ	Ⓑ	Ⓒ	Ⓓ	34.	Ⓐ	Ⓑ	Ⓒ	Ⓓ
10.	Ⓐ	Ⓑ	Ⓒ	Ⓓ	35.	Ⓐ	Ⓑ	Ⓒ	Ⓓ
11.	Ⓐ	Ⓑ	Ⓒ	Ⓓ	36.	Ⓐ	Ⓑ	Ⓒ	Ⓓ
12.	Ⓐ	Ⓑ	Ⓒ	Ⓓ	37.	Ⓐ	Ⓑ	Ⓒ	Ⓓ
13.	Ⓐ	Ⓑ	Ⓒ	Ⓓ	38.	Ⓐ	Ⓑ	Ⓒ	Ⓓ
14.	Ⓐ	Ⓑ	Ⓒ	Ⓓ	39.	Ⓐ	Ⓑ	Ⓒ	Ⓓ
15.	Ⓐ	Ⓑ	Ⓒ	Ⓓ	40.	Ⓐ	Ⓑ	Ⓒ	Ⓓ
16.	Ⓐ	Ⓑ	Ⓒ	Ⓓ	41.	Ⓐ	Ⓑ	Ⓒ	Ⓓ
17.	Ⓐ	Ⓑ	Ⓒ	Ⓓ	42.	Ⓐ	Ⓑ	Ⓒ	Ⓓ
18.	Ⓐ	Ⓑ	Ⓒ	Ⓓ	43.	Ⓐ	Ⓑ	Ⓒ	Ⓓ
19.	Ⓐ	Ⓑ	Ⓒ	Ⓓ	44.	Ⓐ	Ⓑ	Ⓒ	Ⓓ
20.	Ⓐ	Ⓑ	Ⓒ	Ⓓ	45.	Ⓐ	Ⓑ	Ⓒ	Ⓓ
21.	Ⓐ	Ⓑ	Ⓒ	Ⓓ	46.	Ⓐ	Ⓑ	Ⓒ	Ⓓ
22.	Ⓐ	Ⓑ	Ⓒ	Ⓓ	47.	Ⓐ	Ⓑ	Ⓒ	Ⓓ
23.	Ⓐ	Ⓑ	Ⓒ	Ⓓ	48.	Ⓐ	Ⓑ	Ⓒ	Ⓓ
24.	Ⓐ	Ⓑ	Ⓒ	Ⓓ	49.	Ⓐ	Ⓑ	Ⓒ	Ⓓ
25.	Ⓐ	Ⓑ	Ⓒ	Ⓓ	50.	Ⓐ	Ⓑ	Ⓒ	Ⓓ

Signature of the Student & Date of Examination	Signature of the Invigilator & Date of Examination